MAKING AND USING BANNERS

Compiled By
Priscilla Nunnerley
and Ruth Wood

Gazelle
BOOKS

Mill Hill, London NW7 3SA

First published by Gazelle Books 1998.

ISBN 1 899746 08 0

By the same author:
An Army with Banners, published 1982
Banners in His Name, published 1986
Banner Makers to the King, published 1989
Banners Around the World, published 1994

Designed and produced by Gazelle Creative Productions Ltd.
Concorde House, Grenville Place, Mill Hill, London NW7 3SA

Contents

PART 4 Ideas and techniques

Preface

This new edition, *Making and Using Banners*, brings together some of the ideas in the first three books, but also introduces new banners, concepts and accounts gathered recently. We are grateful for all we have received, though inevitably, we have had to be selective. Our aim has been to illustrate a variety of styles and skills.

It is our hope that this edition will provide fresh inspiration for ideas. There is information about new techniques and different types of materials and a section on resources.

Most of the banners pictured are taken by amateur photographers, therefore the book has that home spun feel, whereas many craft books rely on professional photography. The aim is to show how banners can be inspired by the Holy Spirit and how the making of them is a spiritual ministry. Anyone and everyone can take part, without requiring artistic skills or sewing ability, since many other gifts are also involved. Christ can be lifted up not only in the final banner, but also in the process of making it.

There is a place for glorious banners — for extravagance to express our adoration and God's splendour and majesty (He is worthy of our highest skills and the best materials people can find). So, at times, bring out the satins, the silks and the nets, rich colours, jewels and pearls, the gold and silver cords. Banner-making can share the exuberant joy of the Creator.

There is equally a place for simple banners well made but in a short time. If there is a message for the people then it needs to be communicated quickly with labour saving aids such as glue instead of sewing or a technique such as spray painting. These banners can communicate clearly, attractively and effectively.

Most of the photos chosen for the book are a mixture of words and pictures but many attractive banners can be made containing words or pictures only.

Banner-making can be a time for relaxation and joy. 'What you do in word or deed, do all in the Name of the Lord Jesus, giving thanks to God, the Father, through Him' (Colossians 3:17).

"Be still and know that I am God." Psalm 46:10

Acknowledgements

This is a book which belongs to many people. The Fisherfolk, a Christian community from Houston, Texas, enriched worship in our country by their contributions in music and folk art. Inspired by them, Antoinette Neal started our first banner group in Amersham in 1973. We are deeply indebted to her and the community.

For all that has followed — for the joy of knowing many people through banner-making, banner days and correspondence; for contributions, past and present, for articles, pictures, drawings, photos and transparencies — thank you. We are especially grateful for those who have prayed.

We thank Stuart Reid, pastor of the King's Church, Amersham, for his support spanning twenty years. Also thanks to Priscilla's sister Rosas Mitchell for her enthusiasm and encouragement, and the production team at Gazelle Creative Productions Ltd who have helped put *Making and Using Banners* together by incorporating graphics, photographs and editorial features.

The words we would echo down the years are 'My grace is sufficient for you' and 'My strength is made perfect in weakness'. And so to the Lord, who led us all the way, we gladly say, 'To God be the glory!'

Priscilla and Ruth

'To God be the glory!'   *St Monks, Colney Heath, St Albans*

I
Why banners?

An introduction to banners
and banner-making

The many uses of banners

Banners — for quiet meditation; joyful celebration; public proclamation; beautiful decoration. There are so many situations in which banners can be used. Banners can encourage, teach, and evoke worship. They speak of God's creativity, of His involvement with our world. Above all, they speak in words, pictures, or both, of Jesus. His is the Name that is lifted high.

Banners can vary in size; be made out of many different materials; be permanent or temporary; and they can be made by people of all ages.

The power of pictures

In today's world we are surrounded by visual images — in television, films, advertising. These pictures are designed to appeal to us deep down, and to affect the way we think about ourselves, our hopes, aspirations and so on. They create a particular world view.

In a similar but profoundly different way, banners can affect us. They can stimulate us to reflect, to repent, to rejoice, to worship. They can proclaim great truths about God. They can challenge us to see ourselves correctly as they reflect something of the nature of God, His truth, and His purposes.

Jesus himself used visual images — pictures painted in words — to bring his teaching home to people. He asked them to use their imagination to see, for example, a shepherd searching for a lost sheep, a father welcoming home a 'lost' son, the carefree beauty of God's creation. In picturing these scenes of ordinary life, his followers learned deep truths about what God is like and could base their lives on these truths.

The Temple, built by Solomon, was a wonderful tribute by His people to the glory of God. The magnificent building with its use of gold and jewels, of beautiful wood and stones, rich in symbolic detail, pointed people's minds and hearts to God. But it was not the Temple which was to be the focus of attention — it was the fact that the glory of the Lord had 'come down'. In the same way, banners point beyond themselves, providing a setting for worship and reminding us of the presence of the Lord.

Old Testament banners

In the Old Testament the word banner means victory. Banners were used as a rallying point in battle in order to unify the army, as well as giving them a visible reminder of their identity. Banners were both an inspiration and an encouragement. The standard-bearer had a vital role — as long as the banner was still upheld, the fight went on. Moses declared in Exodus 17:15 'the Lord is my banner'. Isaiah writes of the Spirit of the Lord lifting up a standard against the enemy when he comes in like a flood.

These Old Testament banners were the forerunners of the flags and regimental colours used throughout the history of Western Europe. Banners carried on marches by craft guilds and trades unions also continued the tradition. All have a place of pride in the memories of men who marched beneath them.

Hymn-writers in centuries past also used the image of carrying banners:

> 'Stand up, stand up for Jesus, ye soldiers of the Cross,
> Lift high his royal banner, it must not suffer loss.'

They were aware that they were part of the great cosmic struggle, fighting alongside God against unseen powers of wickedness in the spiritual realms. They were under battle orders from the captain of the hosts of heaven.

In a similar way, banners used in procession of witness, such as the international 'March for Jesus' which proclaim Jesus are carrying on this great tradition — the declaration of God's sovereignty in the world He has made.

The risen Christ breaks out of the grave with power and victory reassuring His followers that He is Lord. *The King's Church, Amersham*

The beauty of banners

Beautiful banners help create the right atmosphere for worshipping God. There is room both for extravagant banners and for simple everyday ones. Different churches will create and use different banners at different times. With the Holy Spirit's guidance, the potential for different designs, textures, shapes and colours is only limited by our ingenuity.

In the Bible, the psalmist talks of longing to dwell in the house of the Lord 'to behold His beauty' (Psalm 27:4). Although external beauty is not an essential requirement for worship, it can remind us of the beauty of the Lord. When we consider the amount of thought and expense in making a living-room in our house attractive and welcoming, should we not give care and attention to the place where we meet for worship?

Being in a beautiful place or looking at something beautiful can quicken our senses and open our spirit to joy. To some extent, what we see determines what we become. In some churches, beauty has been denied for too long. Beauty expressed in flowers, music, furnishings, paintings, sculptures, dance and banners

On 25 June 1994 twelve million people in 172 countries went on a *March for Jesus*. Similar marches and prayer walks around the world are planned for the future.

gives us but a glimpse of God's wonder and riches. Let's enjoy them! And let us worship the Lord in them!

The aim of banners

The aim of our banners is to lift the word before the people so they see it, absorb it, meditate on it, remember and obey it. Words portrayed visually can be retained by the memory much longer than the spoken word.

The psalmist says, 'Thy statutes have been my songs in the house of my pilgrimage' (Psalm 119). The word is our delight, our refreshing, our bread, our strength, our light, our guide and our life. The man who meditates on the law of God continually is called blessed (Psalm 1). He is likened to a tree whose roots go down deep into the water and can still bear green leaves in time of drought.

The words of the Bible have the power of no other words. I (Priscilla speaking) have seen a church banner based on some words given in a vision, and although the banner was beautiful and was of help to that particular congregation, it didn't have the universal power of the Word of God.

> A banner must be the means for God to speak and be glorified rather than the artwork.

Look at several versions of the Bible to get the most relevant and expressive words. The words of Scripture and the search for God can be echoed in hymns and these, too, can be used. One banner was made for Whitsun with the words 'Come down, O Love Divine' and they were clear and fitting for that occasion.

Banners in worship

All of His creation is for the glory of God. Our creativity in banners should lead to the same end. The purpose is to convey or recall who He is, what He has done and is doing, and to bring us to worship Him.

The Bible is our true guide to God so that must be the inspiration behind all our designs. Banners are not an alternative to the preaching and reading of God's word, but they can help to break open our predictable thought patterns. They are not simply to give us more information but to stimulate our thinking and stir our imagination, causing us to look at an old story in new ways. The image on a banner enables us to open our eyes to consider the amazing, unchanging truths of God's revelation and the gospel of Jesus Christ. Through banners, as through some fine art and literature, we can gain fresh and helpful insights into the wonder of God and, even beyond that, experience Him for ourselves.

Banners are meant to be 'seen through', not just looked at.

We trust the Holy Spirit to take our eyes beyond the fine needlework, design and craftmanship to contemplate and meditate on the truth represented, leading us to the real world where God is and setting on fire our immortal spirits with love for Him.

Stuart Reid

Made from gold and coloured papers with various printed pictures, each representing a name of Jesus. *Left to right:* Saviour, Lion, Lamb, Bright and Morning Star, Light of the World, the Vine, Alpha and Omega, King of kings. *The King's Church, Amersham*

Using Scripture effectively

To proclaim:
- Jesus is Lord
- God was in Christ
- The free gift of God is eternal life in Christ Jesus

To celebrate:
- The harvest with joy
- The two shall become one
- He is risen

To strengthen and comfort:
- His banner over me is love
- God is faithful
- Nothing shall separate us from the Love of God
- He lives to make intercession

To challenge:
- Watch and pray
- What does the Lord require of you?
- Go into all the world

To command:
- Rejoice in the Lord
- Watch and pray
- Freely you have received; freely give
- Love one another
- Bear ye one another's burdens

To promise:
- I will return
- I will pour my Spirit upon you
- I will come to you
- If we confess our sins, He is faithful and just to forgive us our sins and to cleanse us from all unrighteousness

To command and promise:
- Bring the full tithes and I will open the windows of heaven
- Ask and you will receive
- Seek and you will find
- Knock and it shall be opened unto you.

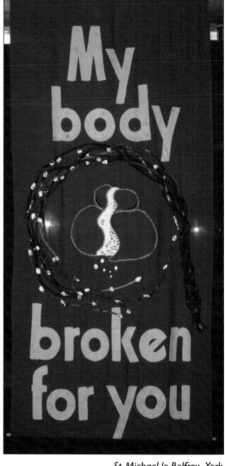

St Michael-le-Belfrey, York

The banner-makers' prayer

Pray that when people see your banner they will not stop at the skill of your handiwork or your inventive design or at the beautiful material, but that all these will be aids to catch their attention, to lead their eye and eventually their heart to the truth you are seeking to express.

Stuart Reid

Using banners in the appropriate context

Banners can be used for a wide variety of purposes, in a number of different situations, for example:

- **Worship and praise** — to help us focus on God
- **Meditation** — to help hear and receive from God
- **Celebration** — baptisms, weddings, anniversaries, festivals and services
- **Comfort** — in difficult times, at funerals, memorials
- **Teaching** — eg, tithing, prayer etc.
- **Decoration** — to bring colour, atmosphere and beauty
- **Creativity** — expressing the artistic and inventive nature of God's people
- **Witness and proclamation** — street marches, prayer walks, outdoor meetings and events etc.

Easter banner (Colossians 1:27).
St Michael-le-Belfrey, York

Making waves: using strong primary colours and rectangular shapes to great effect in a street march. Easy and quick using inexpensive fabric, stitched or stapled around dowel rod.
1996 March for Jesus, London

Banners – a rich experience

Banner-making can be enjoyed by people of all ages and backgrounds. It is a rich experience for a group of people to create something together and offer it to God, knowing that their gift to Him may be used to influence and enrich others. Banners are not an end in themselves. They are a natural outcome of our life in God, leading us on into a deeper knowledge of the Lord and His purposes.

Just as we read in the Old Testament about how God gave creative gifts to his people in order to build the Tabernacle and the Temple, so He is giving gifts in banner-making to His people today. For many people in church, music has a deep significance; in the same way, visual art can have a profound effect. Visual symbolism offers a window through which beauty and the truth of God's word can touch our spirits. As we meditate on the words or design we are drawn beyond ourselves to focus on God.

Banners as a focal point in a hired room are of great value. Here the banner (with the cross beautifully embroidered by Kath Goward) hangs on a mirror in an old banqueting hall (called the gold room) in a mansion.

Wendy Toller, Goring New Life Baptist Church, Worthing

Banners speak to the spirit through the eyes. A good banner must arrest attention and draw people to stop and look. Symbols and colours communicate to the senses and through the senses to the spirit. It is therefore important that a banner is more than someone's 'good idea': it must come through revelation from the Holy Spirit.

Responding to God with the inspiration of banners

- Ask the Holy Spirit to speak to you through the banner
- Seek the main message of the banner
- Ponder on the words, chew them over, ask God to help you
- Ask 'How does this apply to my life?'
- Let God speak to you
- See yourself in your imagination enjoying the good of that truth
- Desire what you have pictured with all your heart
- Remind yourself of it daily from your Bible or from memory
- Ask the Holy Spirit to confirm this vision in your heart (see Mark 11:24)
- Wait in thankfulness, until you see its outworking in your life.

Stuart Reid

2
Banner groups

In this part we look at starting a group, the value of being part of a group, the role of the leader, how to plan a banner, banner workshops, and some personal accounts of banner projects

Starting a banner group

Whereas beautiful banners are made by individuals, there is something very special in working as a group and creating a banner together. Paul reminded the Christians at Corinth that God gives individual people gifts in order to build up the whole church. When we use our creative gifts together, several principles emerge:

- Prayer is answered when two or three pray in Jesus' name.

- The different abilities of the group to make a rich and more varied whole.

- The ideas of one person can be confirmed and checked by others. Ideas can be sifted, worked out and sometimes rejected.

- Talents and skills are developed as we appreciate and encourage one another. Sometimes abilities emerge that one never realised one possessed.

- One learns to give and take, to overcome fears and lack of confidence, to forgo cherished ideas in the interests of the group and to grow in confidence and love.

- People working together as a group have fellowship, fun, sharing and discussion about many topics as they stitch and stick.

Anyone can take part

Any Christian can take part in making banners because the making of them is primarily a spiritual ministry, so artistic ability is not necessarily a requirement. This cannot be too heavily emphasised. Those who are new to the idea and join a small group can start by cutting out letters and sewing hems and so contribute to a bigger project.

Natural talents offered to the Lord are touched and then transformed to become a spiritual gift to glorify God and build up the body of Christ.

Gill Douglas comments: 'We can only give to the world as much as we have amongst ourselves. As we share our lives within our groups in love and commitment so, like the alabaster box of ointment broken open so that the perfume could flow, we too are broken and God's fragrance is set free in our churches and in the world. The quality of our banner is a direct reflection of where we are with God and with each other. We can have lovely designs and beautiful craftsmanship, but the resulting banners can be empty unless we have the right foundations. Our willingness to allow God to work in our relationships allows His Spirit to flow. As we draw close to Him and to each other so He is able to speak to us and anoint our gifts.'

Steps to making a banner

Here are some guidelines which you might want to use when you have formed your banner group. You will find detailed information on the practical 'how to' aspects of banner-making in Parts Three and Four of this book.

Kelsall Banner Group (Tarporley, Cheshire) share in the making of a harvest banner.

Prayer
Praying together and asking God to guide you through the project is essential.

Questions
What is the message we want to convey?
Will this be a straightforward banner or one which will take several weeks?

Early planning stages
1. You need ideas and inspiration. Meditate on a verse or short passage from the Bible. The book of Psalms is a good place to start.
2. Decide on the words and/or design. This may take more than one session.
3. Choose the lettering — make sure it matches the 'mood' of the banner.
4. Decide on background colour, technique, etc.
5. Assign someone to buy fabric and materials.
6. Arrange times to meet , how often — and a workable completion date!

During the making
Involve everyone in the project. If there are more than six of you, you may need to meet in two groups. Enjoy the friendship and the fun. The relationships will last when the banners are tattered remnants!

Gill Sathy explains how to get started

If you are thinking about starting a banner group you may feel you do not know how to go about it or perhaps you lack the courage to take the plunge. If you are in this stage of mind, trust in the Lord, cast fear aside and go ahead.

All you need is enthusiasm and a desire to create something for God and his people — for God will help you to overcome the obstacles or difficulties you feel might hold you back.

I wanted to do something artistic for years. I wasn't sure what I wanted to do until I went to a 'Banner Day'. I was overwhelmed by the beauty of the banners I saw that day: some were very simple, some were decorative, but they were all done with praying hands and love for Jesus. The day of fellowship and sharing fired me with enthusiasm.

After that I spent a great deal of time in praying and thinking about the formation of a banner group and in searching the Scriptures for texts which could be used on banners. It was an important time for me — learning to wait on the Lord, and to submit everything to Him in prayer.

Meanwhile I made a simple harvest banner on my own. It was oats against a red sun and I used fabric paints and pens. I learned a few of the intricacies of banner-making in the process.

Eventually the idea of banner-making as an aid to worship was launched at church through a talk during the Sunday evening service. The next evening an introductory meeting was held and, much to my surprise, eleven people came. We had a lovely evening together. A friend gave us some handy tips and good ideas. I had prepared a list of twelve texts which could be used for Christmas banners. We briefly discussed these, and decided to make four banners. Each person was given a copy of the twelve texts to take home in order to decide the four best and draw designs for them if they wished to.

The first meeting of the banner group took place the following week. We began our meeting with a short time of prayer and meditation to quieten our minds and feel the presence of God. The whole meeting went off very smoothly and many important decisions were reached. We chose the four texts and four designs, and the size of lettering. We decided to have one evening and an afternoon group as there were too many of us to meet together. It was only after I reached home that I realised that one design had been chosen from every one of the four people who brought along designs. My heart was full with praise and thanksgiving.

The words which I had read out at the beginning of the meeting were from Exodus 23:20-21: 'See I am sending an angel ahead of you to guard you along the way and to bring you to a place I have prepared. Pay attention to him and listen to what he says!' These words were true for us that night and for all our other meetings. We listened to our Lord, and He directed us in the paths we should walk.

There is a price to pay for starting a banner group. It does not just involve the group meetings. You need time for thinking and praying; time to prepare; time to buy; time to do sewing not completed in the meetings; time to get all the necessary equipment together before each meeting. Do not be afraid to take a few weeks off after the completion of a banner or series of banners. You — and your family — will need a rest from them — as sometimes you will find that the banners take over your life! Starting and running a banner group does take a lot of time and effort. However, I am just grateful and happy that the Lord has given me this job to do.   *Gill Sathy*

Leading a group

The leader is a person who not only has the vision for making and using banners in the church but also one who can organize the group, setting dates and goals.

Some groups do not have a leader — it is possible to work well together, making a banner for a special project, for example, and not need a leader, but merely depending on someone who can co-ordinate the group. Other groups work better with a leader who has a clearly defined role. It is more important for a leader to be able to encourage others to make and create than to dominate the group with their own ideas.

Ideas for banners

These can come in so many ways — a flash of inspiration, an idea that grows, something that arises out of meditation by the whole group as they read the Bible together, the response of the group to a particular situation or circumstance. Ideas for banners can come slowly and step-by-step, with each member of the group contributing, and different people making and suggesting different parts.

Inspiration comes from the Holy Spirit's guidance while the group is at work; from each individual's walk with the Lord; from listening to what He is saying; through prayer; in a time of worship together. There is one group which spends three sessions in Bible study before they spend seven sessions making a set of banners. Each group is different, and will need to find its own way forward.

How to find inspiration and get ideas is discussed in more detail in Part Three.

Margery's story

Margery hates sewing and is not naturally artistic but has a banner as a wall-hanging in her home. Once she shared with others how it came to be made. She said: 'I felt we should

A good leader

- Encourages — helps people discover their gifts;
- Is a catalyst — a channel of the Holy Spirit to others;
- Directs — sets deadlines well before the date;
- Lets go his/her own interests and allows others to create;
- Develops other people's gifts and recognises their skills;
- Cares for people in the group, supports them in prayer;
- Takes responsibility for the project stage by stage, improves, adjusts;
- Refuses ideas that are not acceptable, but sees each member has a part to play;
- Guides the conversation away from negative thinking, grumbling and criticism;
- Helps everyone to see the potential for creativity in others, helps the group to believe and desire the best of, and for each other.

have a banner in our home so that as people come in they know the Lord is here. My husband, Bruce, liked the idea. I phoned a friend and arranged a meeting to discuss it. I sat down on the settee and wondered what to do. The words came into my mind:

"You shall love the Lord your God
with all your heart, with all your soul
and with all your strength"

'These words tell us that our love for Him must come first.

'I went to the meeting thrilled that the Lord had given me inspiration for this banner. It cost hardly anything to make. The background material is curtain fabric, left over from the living room curtains. The flowers are cut from another fabric. The only thing I bought was the felt. How it's helped me as I've passed it in the hall. It's been a constant reminder to put God first!'

Margery stayed with the group for nearly two years. By her very presence she made the most important contribution, that of herself. Along with some encouragement and help she was drawn into cutting single letters and stitching, choosing, purchasing and gluing. We shared our lives and got to know each other and that was, perhaps, more important than the banners we made.

This banner simply conveys the lonely figure of Jesus on the Cross with the profound words 'Such Love'.

Biggin Hill Christian Fellowship, Kent

Two elaborate Easter banners contrasting the grief of the crucifixion and the brightness and joy of the resurrection. Notice how colour conveys mood and atmosphere.

St Martins, Barnehurst, Kent

Kelsall banner group tell their story

Kelsall banner group started in 1992, at Kelsall Methodist Church, Tarporley, Cheshire. There are twelve active members, and a number of helpful husbands and supporters. The group does not have a leader; all share in the ideas for banners and the planning often takes longer than the making. We discovered a wide variety of skills in the group, and one of the great pleasures has been the way in which we have learned techniques from one another and discovered one another's talents. The use of a quilting frame makes it possible for four or five to work together at the 'sewing-on' stage.

The decision to make two small banners rather than one big one arose from the fact that the Christmas tree stands in front of the wall where our larger banners usually hang. We decided to make a pair, for either side of the pulpit, in such a way that they could also hang side by side in another setting. The words, Gaze in Wonder, and Kneel in Homage, come from the hymn 'Come and Join the Celebration'. The dominant star is made from layers of silver mesh and net. We used rich fabrics for the kings, and plain ones for the shepherds, all rag-bag materials, and took a lot of care to try to make the posture of the people look natural. There are lots of sparkly stars and lights in the windows of 'Bethlehem' which catch the lights at dark winter evening services.

The Easter banner

Margaret Morton of the banner group at Chalfont St Giles Fellowship tells the story of their Easter banner project

E aster was nearly upon us and there seemed so much to do and as usual so little time to do it in. Palm Sunday, The Last Supper, Good Friday and Easter Sunday — we needed four banners. We prayed, we had looked at Scriptures and then realised that the solution was a very easy one. The Cross said it all. Why not one banner depicting each of the four aspects?

We all met in Gerrards Cross at our usual shop, where the assistants have been so helpful and encouraging, to choose our materials. We chose rough hessian for the cross, soft silks for the leaves for Palm Sunday and gold reflective materials for the cup representing the Last Supper.

> We prayed, we had looked at Scriptures and then realised that the solution was a very easy one. The Cross said it all. Why not one banner depicting each of the four aspects.

What we needed

We bought, for the crown of thorns, a circle of thin interwoven flexible twigs to which some brown felt cut with jagged edges was sewn.

The elements of the banner were now complete, the pieces tacked on and then machined in gold, red and blue silk. Each quadrant overlapped part of the cross — all of them essential parts making up the Easter story.

1 Palm Sunday in the top left-hand corner has sweeping leaves in different green silks; a gold thread runs through the centre, depicting Christ's Kingship.

2 The Last Supper in the top right-hand corner — the gold cup is slightly tilted with the wine spilling out (sewn on in red sequins). The broken bread was quite hard to portray. Some tight-covered wadding slit in the centre proved very effective.

3 The Cross is central to the Easter story and to this banner. Each quadrant of the Easter story overlaps a little onto the Cross. The crown of thorns quadrant was a very vivid portrayal — translucent purples, oranges, blues and reds trying to explain the battles of Kingship, sacrifice and judgement.

4 The empty tomb was a peaceful scene — calm beige, green grass but bright gold and triumphal skies. The cross was left plain, the simplicity of His sacrifice clearly and unmistakably shown — death on our behalf which enables us to have a relationship with the King of kings.

1

2

3

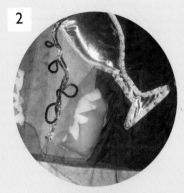

4

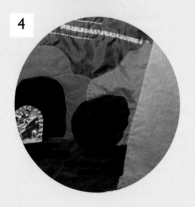

Above: The completed banner

Left: Detail of the Easter banner shows the mixed use of fabric, stitching and appliqué to achieve an enduring three dimensional image. See how the cross holds the composition together. You can trace or adapt this, adding your own ideas, materials and colours. For the very ingenious, the elements could be illuminated from behind or from the front using well-placed spotlights.

Banner workshops

One way in which a larger group can operate is to meet for a longer time on a Saturday. Here they can share ideas, receive teaching, pray and worship together — and make banners!

The leader brings:

- visual aids, perhaps based on a theme (eg grapes, an ear of corn)
- a variety of Bibles, including Good News with the pictures
- glue
- box of cottons, threads, silks, wool, etc
- old necklaces, assorted beads, coloured and gold cords
- background fabrics
- pieces of felt
- scraps of material
- cotton wool for padding
- sequins
- net and tulle
- leather
- fur fabric
- iron and ironing board
- sewing machine

Group members bring:

- Bible
- paper, pencils etc
- sewing kit
- scissors
- materials

How one church spent their day

10am   Talk on banner-making with many examples.

11am   Coffee followed by open prayer. The theme was announced — 'The words of Jesus about nature.' Ten suggestions had been prepared on slips of paper — vine, water, wild flowers, corn and so on. Each had one or two Bible references. People divided into five groups with four in each and chose one of the suggestions, so each group did something different. Then they sat round a table meditating on the Bible verses, discussing and drawing ideas. Before lunch some people had chosen background fabrics and started cutting out shapes.

3.30pm   An industrious happy afternoon concluded. Because of further stitching etc that needed to be done, a date was set three weeks ahead when the banners would be hung in church.

A banner day for several churches

A gathering of people from different churches can meet together. This is an account of one such event.

We met in our chapel on a Saturday. Most people had already made banners and brought some along. There were so many hanging from every possible nail and rail that we were almost submerged! We started with praise and then heard a talk on the name of Jesus. Then eight people shared their work and experiences. Some had been asked to talk about specific topics such as machine embroidery, batik, and craft materials and others spoke more generally. The day finished with a lively discussion.

Another way would have been to spend the afternoon in practical sessions with different people sharing their skills and leading their groups in some activity.

This sort of event is an opportunity for people to meet each other and enjoy the banners displayed, and a good hour or more at lunch time will make this possible.

Rosas Mitchell leading a discussion seminar at a banner day in the Murray Place Baptist Church in Stirling, Scotland.

Creating a Christmas banner

Ruth Wood leads a workshop at Charlton Kings, Cheltenham

Our morning session in the church had been an opportunity for the group to get to know each other, and to think in general about banners. We moved to a smaller room for the practical session and sat together round a table with paper and pencils. The aim was to plan a banner for Christmas.

We started with prayer and then had a reading and meditation on Matthew 2:1–12.

One of the group immediately knew which words should be used. 'They rejoiced with exceeding great joy' (I had no idea they had stood out as I read). Another lady had the picture — a star and rejoicing figures.

After discussion several changes were made. The magi became modern figures, 'exceeding' was altered to 'great' and 'they rejoiced' to the injunction 'rejoice'.

It became obvious that there should be three banners instead of one — panels of words on either side of the picture, fitting well the rather large sculptured area of the church wall. The workshop had been a model of people working creatively and thoughtfully with each other.

3

Designing and using your banner

In this part we explore the ways in which we can find inspiration; the use of colour, composition, lettering and shape. We also look at the finished result of various kinds of banners

The task of being creative

Priscilla Nunnerley shares some of her experiences

The struggle produced between the germ of an idea and its final out-working can be called creative tension. The tension in banner-making comes when one takes the initial concept and tries to work it out in material terms.

Here is an account of one banner I made.

Marjorie and I were the only two at that planning session for the Christmas banners. However, we were sure of the words. We had pondered on them for two weeks and our pastor, Stuart, had independently suggested them. 'Wonderful Counsellor, Mighty God, Everlasting Father and Prince of Peace.' He'd scribbled away to show us a sketch. 'Get out a library book about illuminated letters — Lindisfarne Gospels, Book of Kells.' Reflecting on these great words of Isaiah, we decided on four parchment-like scrolls.

Damp used tea-leaves are an invaluable aid to the making of the parchment type background. So we spread the leaves over 2-metre lengths of wallpaper (reverse side), left them to dry and then removed them. (You can give your paper a bath in cold tea!)

The busier you are, the more you need to pray, so, conscious of the task ahead, I got myself down to the women's prayer meeting. Sharing our need for inspiration, I

said that we were undertaking to do these illuminated letters, the originals of which took monks a life-time. When the prayer time concluded, Katie and Vicky offered to join us. We all went back to my place and started working on the letters. Marjorie worked on the lower case letters and the rest of us on capitals. Katie completed four of the eight letters. We all took work home to continue during the week.

> It is good to get away to think and meditate on the task and to allow God to speak. As you observe His creation, it is wonderful to rediscover the amazing intricacies of design, colour, reflections of light and pattern which can provide fresh inspiration.

There was one other banner: the focus of Christmas. It was my task to work on the name 'Jesus'. See banner on page 11. I found this to be the greatest source of joy of any creative task I have ever undertaken, but it was also a spiritual struggle. All the week I'd had a sense of heaviness, and on the following evening I was so unhappy I went to talk to a friend. Explaining the project to her I suggested this cloud on my spirit was an attack from the powers of darkness because I was working on the name 'Jesus'. She reminded me that the Bible promises that if Jesus is lifted up He will draw all men unto Himself. The power in the raising of His name could be hated by the enemy. She prayed for deliverance and protection. I returned to continue the task, still struggling but with the weight on my spirit gone.

We decided that the name of 'Jesus' should be in capitals, so I cut these out in large pale yellow paper letters. Plain gold-coloured letters, made of thin card, identical in shape but slightly smaller, were placed on top of each yellow letter, so allowing a contrasting border to show. Trying to invent some decoration around and inside the letters, I cut up old Christmas cards to see if they would fit. Suddenly, after long hours, an idea came. I could represent the names of Jesus pictorially. Inspiration from the Lord can sometimes be so clear. As I continued I had a sense of standing apart, watching the idea grow.

I did not have the ability to paint the pictures, but I had recently bought a greeting card of a lion's head. This would represent the Lion of the Tribe of Judah. The regal yet warm face of the lion was closely linked in my mind with the Aslan of C. S. Lewis' *Narnia* books. The picture fitted into the upper part of the letter 'E'. Below it fitted a picture of a lamb taken from a child's Ladybird book. A photograph of Earth taken from the moon provided 'The Light of the World', and one of the night sky with a silver star added was 'The Bright and Morning Star'. A poster of a vine was slipped into the centre of the 'U'. The 'J' provided a niche for the picture of the Saviour in the manger. The last letter remained. I cut a yellow card 'Alpha' and 'Omega' and also a red and gold crown for the parts of the 'S'.

> Ultimately, all our work will be an act of faith — the responsiveness of hearts humble enough to accept correction but eager to obey His commission (Matthew 28:19) and to share Him. Without such faith it is impossible to please Him.

The pleasure of doing this remained with me for days. The near ecstasy of knowing the inspiration came from the Lord and yet being His mind and hands for the outworking of it, was the greatest joy in anything I have ever made.

Speak, for your servant is listening (various contributors)

Sometimes we ask ourselves, 'Does God want us to make banners, and if so, can we know precisely what He wants us to do? Are we really hearing from Him?' I believe the Lord has a way of letting us know what He wants us to do. The Lord delights to speak. He has promised us His Holy Spirit to guide us into all truth. Our task in banner-making is to seek and knock. If we believe that God sends His word forth to accomplish a specific goal, we must enquire of Him for each specific assignment. We must pray that He will illuminate our minds so that we may choose a word that is timely and fitting and will prove of real blessing.

Some banners need to be simple. There are many banners such as those made quickly for the church, for processions or for small gifts, that do not need the thought and prayer that is given to the more weighty and magnificent creations! Many times I have just got on and made a banner with words from the Word of God because I wanted to do so.

Hearing together

It does not follow that hearing from God as a group is more difficult than hearing him on your own. For a start, many banners will be straightforward. You do not need a long discussion on 'Praise the Lord', except perhaps on the practical details! Bible verses or phrases of proclamation, praise and promise which are constant and universal statements are appropriate at any time of the year.

Other banners do require special thought. Gill Douglas writes: 'In recent years, banner groups have become increasingly aware of their role in seeking the Lord for a word that is on His heart. We have desired to capture His love, might and majesty and to receive a message from Him, from the Word of God, that will direct us ahead — a "now" (or *rhema* word).'

Sometimes the text is given with a request for a banner. For instance, a friend wanted a banner made and had several verses which she knew were suitable. She came along to the group for the evening to help us select a few words from these.

Other times, somebody may have suggested a suitable text for a new banner. Meeting together, the group has prayed and considered these words to see if we agree. I have twice taken along what I thought were appropriate texts, but they were not required! We acknowledge that the Lord leads us very clearly in the choice of His word and it really does become a rallying point and a standard for His people.

Meditating on the task

We sometimes meet without any preconceived words or designs. We state the purposes for which we've come together, and spend some time in extempore or silent prayer. We then meditate on the task and eventually scriptures come to mind — sometimes just one clear word. We then have an hour discussing ideas and words, designs and colours. We usually finish with some definite ideas and come to the next meeting able to start the background and design letters. Two to seven practical sessions follow.

When the group has a sense of rightness about certain words then those are the ones. The knowledge is an inner witness to the Holy Spirit speaking. You can sense Him, but He is like the wind and you can't predict or direct Him.

Some examples of other ways in which we have worked together to hear what the Lord wants us to say: the group has a Bible study; others in the church contribute ideas: maybe a pastor or leader; relevant objects or music are used to stimulate thought — songs, hymns, poems, extracts, photographs, pictures.

Murray Place Baptist Church, Stirling, Scotland

A certain banner group usually sketches ideas on paper and then puts them all out on the table to consider. They often find a common theme coming through. If, on the odd occasion, someone disagrees, they pray and rethink the design.

If there is any question or doubt, ask for the Holy Spirit's confirmation, maybe by seeking your pastor's advice. One group, on meeting to make a Christmas banner, could not decide on anything and so felt the Lord wanted them to have more time for other things at that busy season.

Our aim is to hear from God for our banners so that others may listen to Him as they look at them. A young man told the pastor that he wanted to become a Christian and, when asked what it was that spoke to him, said that it was an Easter banner, 'Behold I am alive for evermore'.

Colour and its effect

Evelyn Lucas of the King's Church, Amersham

Choosing colours and texture is an essential part of making a banner. While colour can affect the viewer for the good and be a form of therapy, it can also have an adverse effect. A large area of bright, intense, garish colour may convey happiness to most people, but it may disturb a few. Similarly, a drab banner can have a very negative effect. The colours chosen may also have suited the theme of the banner, but the result may be different from what was originally intended.

Colour relationships

Consult one of the many art and needlework books with a colour section and you will be amazed at the range of possibilities. For example, experiment by placing a green square on a larger magenta square and then place the green square on a different green. **1** You will see that the two opposing colours appear bright and intense while **2** two similar colours seem to cancel one another out.

Sometimes it is pleasing to use different shades of the same colour but it can also produce a dull result. **3** A small amount of red close to the centre of focus can often bring such a banner to life and draw the viewer to the focal point. Try to decide in the planning stage where your centre of focus is going to be and your main colour scheme. Everything else should be subservient to this decision — don't overdo it, but be aware of it.

Choosing colour schemes

Colour is a highly individual thing: some people prefer bright definite colours; others choose softer muted shades. Blues

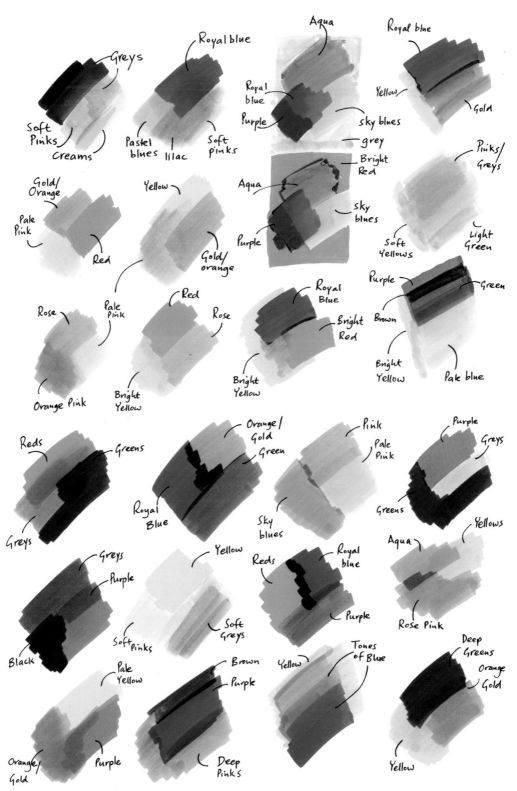

Greys

Royal blue

Aqua

Royal blue

Soft Pinks

Creams

Pastel blues   lilac   Soft pinks

Royal blue

Purple

sky blues

grey

Yellow

Gold

Gold/Orange

Pale Pink

Red

Yellow

Gold/orange

Aqua

Bright Red

Purple

sky blues

Pinks/Greys

Soft Yellows

Light Green

Rose

Pale Pink

Red

Rose

Royal Blue

Bright Red

Purple

Green

Brown

Bright Yellow

Pale blue

Orange Pink

Bright Yellow

Bright Yellow

Reds

Greens

Greys

Greys

Orange/Gold

Green

Royal Blue

Pink

Pale Pink

Sky blues

Purple

Greys

Greens

Yellows

Greys

Purple

Black

Yellow

Soft Pinks

Soft Greys

Reds

Royal blue

Purple

Aqua

Rose Pink

Orange/Gold

Pale Yellow

Purple

Brown

Purple

Deep Pinks

Yellow

Tones of Blue

Yellow

Deep Greens

Orange/Gold

Yellow

and greens have a restful effect, though blue can be a cold colour, particularly in a north-facing room. Bright reds and yellows are attractive to some but others find them loud and disturbing. However you choose your colours, you need to think of the context of your banner — where it will hang.

Colour can be used to create a 3-D effect. For example, hills will appear blue/grey from a distance rather than green. Use this knowledge to create depth.

If your emphasis is on words, use a soft background and a stronger colour for letters. But if the picture is to tell the story, then reduce the colour in the words. It is often useful for a banner group to hold a session where you just look at colours and experiment with them, or invite an artist to talk about the effective use of colour.

Some comments on the use of colour:

'Churches with bright banners, telling of God's love and care in Christ's death, make me feel so different. I don't need to struggle because the banner conveys the fact that the battle has been won already. So a banner in lovely colours can lift my spirit and bring me warmth and joy.' *Yvonne Brooks*

'Colour creates the mood — atmosphere, light, darkness, warmth, cold, friction and conflict and Majesty. There are no set rules regarding the use of colour in banner making but the too liberal use of colour can destroy the impact of what could be a purposeful banner.' *George Holden*

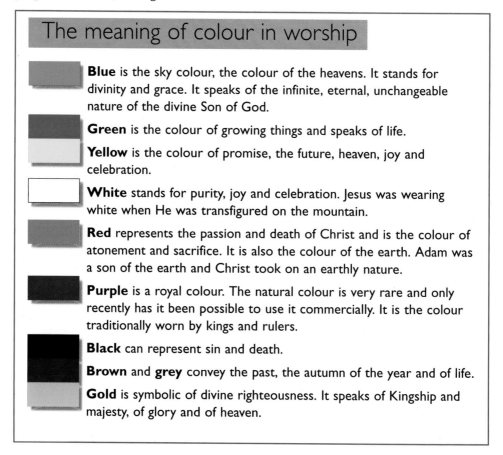

The meaning of colour in worship

Blue is the sky colour, the colour of the heavens. It stands for divinity and grace. It speaks of the infinite, eternal, unchangeable nature of the divine Son of God.

Green is the colour of growing things and speaks of life.

Yellow is the colour of promise, the future, heaven, joy and celebration.

White stands for purity, joy and celebration. Jesus was wearing white when He was transfigured on the mountain.

Red represents the passion and death of Christ and is the colour of atonement and sacrifice. It is also the colour of the earth. Adam was a son of the earth and Christ took on an earthly nature.

Purple is a royal colour. The natural colour is very rare and only recently has it been possible to use it commercially. It is the colour traditionally worn by kings and rulers.

Black can represent sin and death.

Brown and **grey** convey the past, the autumn of the year and of life.

Gold is symbolic of divine righteousness. It speaks of Kingship and majesty, of glory and of heaven.

Inspiration from everyday life

It was a magic moment in the dim interior of an old French abbey. Suddenly I saw brilliant circles of colour, blue and green, red, orange and yellow, dancing on the old grey stone floor. The slate grey background was a superb foil to the brilliance of colour that was summer sunshine coming through a high stained-glass window.

The background colour is important. It serves as a contrast in order to show up the designs and letters to the best advantage. With light designs, a dark or rich colour may be best as a background. With bold or darker designs, a light background would be most suitable. If you already have some fabric, stand at a distance from it and judge which colour, designs and letters would be best.

Do not be afraid to be bold. Too many designs are not seen clearly because the background is a nondescript colour that provides no contrast. Consider choosing a colour that will fit in with the meaning (see box on *the meaning of colour in worship*), but do not feel bound by this.

Sometimes consider more unusual colours such as wine, apricot, rust and clover. Conversely, a piece of fabric will inspire an idea. For example, sea-green, a fishing design and deep blue, a night sky.

Designing your banner

Clare Ashburner, The King's Church, Amersham

Once the words and the concept are confirmed by the Holy Spirit, it is time to design. It is important not to hurry this stage, as time spent perfecting the design will reap benefits in the excellence of the finished banner.

Take a large sheet of paper and a soft pencil — 3-6B — and start doodling. This is not to show whether or not you can draw, but to prove to yourselves that you have thought about what you are planning and have considered alternatives.

Play around with ideas, magazine cuttings or some of the banners in this book, and don't confine yourself to accepting the first idea that comes to mind. Imagine new ways of seeing your concept, and roughly sketch them out, remembering that this is not the time to go into great detail. This is a good opportunity for seeking the inspiration which you may well be given.

Consider your commission; is there a best size and shape for the place where the banner is to hang? Measure and draw four or more small rectangles 5 x 7 inches (10 x 15 cms) or other appropriate shapes roughly to scale and place your various ideas in them.

The words must be incorporated at this stage as part of the design. As the words are important let them stand out well by the significance of the space around them, not just by their size.

Finally you can go on to a more detailed drawing in an enlarged version.

> A simple design is often very much more effective than a cluttered fussy one. The impact of the design must be immediate.
>
> *Rachel McHugh*

Remember that banners with life-giving words, excellently designed and worked, will always be a blessing.

AVOID	ASSESS
• Too many symbols in one banner. The result is confusing.	• The space available to hang the banner. This affects choice of shape, colour and size. Can you see it from the back of the building?
• Small symbols or designs that give a bitty impression. Blend in the words to give a unified effect.	• Whether the shape is appropriate for the design and lettering.
• Designs that are too complex or cannot be seen at a distance.	• If the materials you choose are appropriate to the design.

Too many different symbols.

Disjointed picture with unconnected symbols.

Words not clear enough.

At last! A design that can be bold, colourful and fun!

TIPS There are some important things to keep in mind:

- **Be clear.** Don't overload the design with 'significant' ideas.
- **Be simple.** Beauty is the absence of superfluity.
- **Be subtle.** Don't feel bound to state the obvious but leave room in the observer's mind to fill in the gaps.

Shapes and sizes

The site chosen will determine the banner shape and size. A large building demands a banner clearly visible from the back. It is essential to choose a shape that enhances the design and lettering and suits its environment and lighting conditions. Some shapes may emphasise the meaning. A festive theme might merit an elaborate shape with a fringe and perhaps tassles. A more solemn subject or an everyday banner could use a simple rectangular shape.

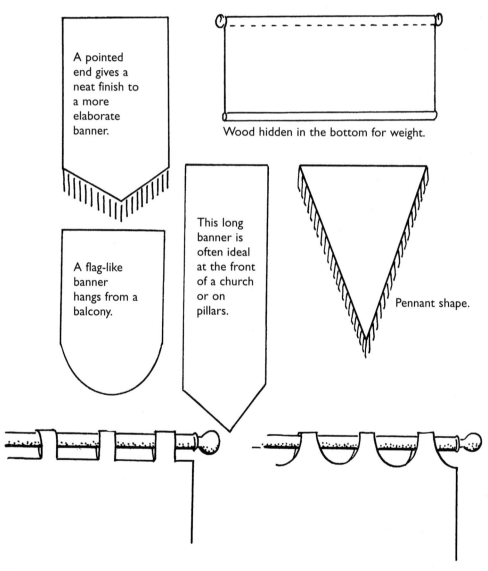

A pointed end gives a neat finish to a more elaborate banner.

Wood hidden in the bottom for weight.

A flag-like banner hangs from a balcony.

This long banner is often ideal at the front of a church or on pillars.

Pennant shape.

Wooden or brass curtain rods and finials (end pieces) are appropriate for permanent banners (See page 92 for display ideas).

Experimenting with lettering

Clare Ashburner

We are very accustomed to reading excellently designed lettering from magazines. As the words on our banners are important, there is also a need for excellence, though many banners tend to fall short at this point. Here are some guidelines for success!

Lettering should be seen as an integral part of the design, not added as an afterthought in the largest available space. It needs a real place of its own where it has room to breathe.

The letters must be the right proportion and size in relation to the banner design.

They should be a coherent style, in keeping with their message or mood.

Spacing is vitally important. As a general rule keep the letters as close together as possible without actually crowding them.

Make sure that the 'weight' of the letters is consistent.

Lower case letters are always easier to read THAN UPPER CASE WHEN THERE ARE SEVERAL WORDS TOGETHER.

Words placed horizontally are more comfortable to read than vertical ones.

The message of the words often comes across better when the words follow on from each other rather than being spread across a design in ones and twos.

Use a grid of lines to get the right proportional size for individual letters.

Often the drafting of the letters is not done until the banner is well advanced. As long as the designated space is still there, this is quite all right. At this stage, rectangles of paper roughly proportional to the letter size (narrower for 'I' wider for 'w') can be laid on the banner to ascertain the actual size needed before each letter is drawn.

Learn the basic disciplines for lettering from books on typography (see *Resources* section at the end of this book for examples). One member of a group might feel led to make a special study of lettering design, or another to try experimenting using a computer with fonts and graphics software program (see next two pages), some might collect illustrations and examples, though all hands are needed to make and sew!

Always get someone else to check the spelling!

There is more detail on how to transfer your design and enlarge lettering, and which materials to use in Part 4: Ideas and techniques, pages 63–70.

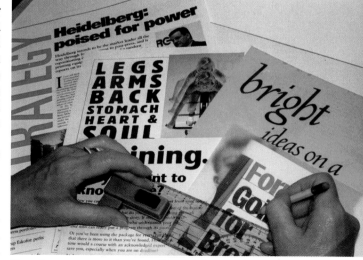

Magazines are a good source for typefaces and layout ideas.

Experiments with lettering using a computer

Praise the Lord

1 The chosen words.

Praise
the Lord

2 Arranging lines.

P r a i s e
t h e
Lord

3 Varying size and spacing giving emphasis to "Lord".

Praise
the
Lord

4 Integrating letters and creating movement.

Praise
the
LORD

5 Keeping it simple.

Praise
the Lord

6 Changing font to a script is fine but watch out that it doesn't prove too fiddly to cut out and stitch, let alone see from a distance.

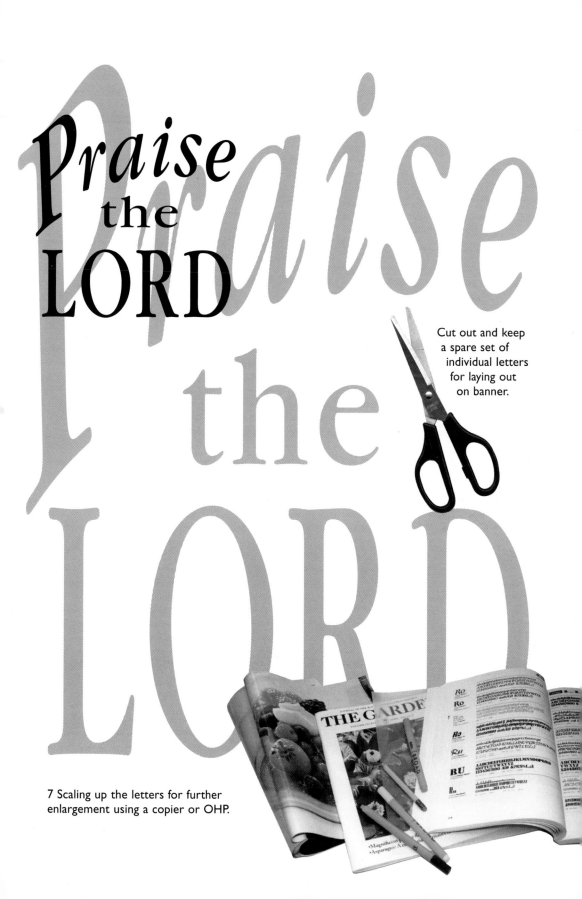

Praise the LORD

Cut out and keep
a spare set of
individual letters
for laying out
on banner.

7 Scaling up the letters for further
enlargement using a copier or OHP.

Banner gallery

This word was worked as a cover for the Lord's Table, celebrating the birth of our Saviour. The letters are gold lamé on a blue poplin background. Each letter is decorated with an embroidered or appliquéd design to give both a seasonal and spiritual message.

The Church of the Holy Spirit, Bedgrove, Aylesbury

This banner was made for a school hall used for our worship on Sunday mornings. The transparent background lets the sun shine through. Real leaves were used to cut fabric leaves. The background is metallic organza. See Resources, p 94 (Borovicks).

The King's Church, Amersham

Four and five-year-old children drew this banner under the leadership of Shirley who had taught them that Jesus is with them. The children were asked to do a drawing of themselves doing some of the things they enjoyed. They then stuck the shapes of material that were cut for them on to the paper drawings and these were glued to hessian. *St Michael-le-Belfrey, York*

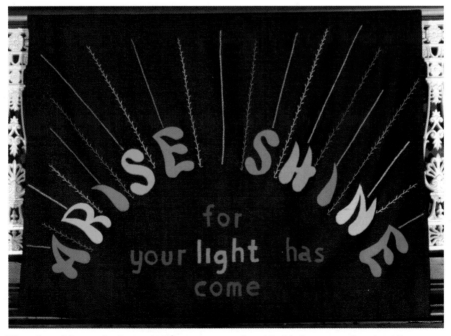

This cheerful straight forward banner was made with felt letters and embroidery stitches and hung in our church at Christmas. *The King's Church, Amersham*

The words are taken from Revelation 19:16, the magnificent passage that describes Christ, the mighty 'Word of God' coming on a white horse with all the armies of heaven behind Him. The letters are gold cord overstitched.   *The King's Church, Amersham*

A drawing from the Good News Bible for Psalm 126:5 inspired this picture. The sheaves are made from knitting wool.

The King's Church, Amersham

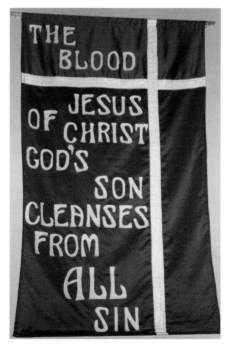

This banner was sent as a gift to a Bible College in South India.

These are mobile banners so that people can group around them to pray. They are made with spray paints and fabric pens on calico. The letters are attached with bondaweb and ironed over greaseproof paper.

Made by Mags Hill of New Life Church, Woking, who likes an instant approach to banner-making

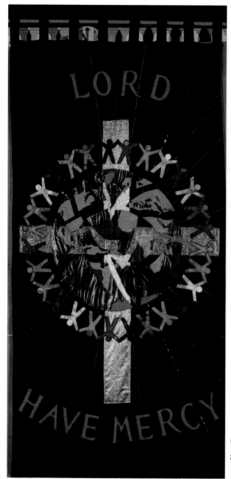

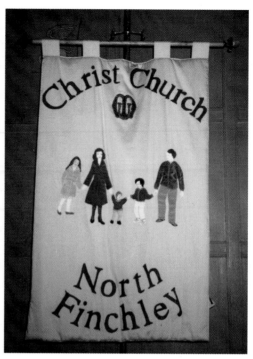

Above: One of a great number of well-made banners on display in North Finchley C of E.

God's people binding together a broken world.
St Michael's-le-Belfry, York

The background is made with spray paint and the ears of corn are felt. If words are required there could be a separate banner.
New Life Church, Durrington, Worthing

The rich, vibrant colours are achieved with fabric paint on material. The letters are silver and gold leathercloth and the figure is made of materials.

St Paul's, Howell Hill, Cheam, Surrey

What kind of soil are you? This was made by the Christchurch, West Croydon banner group at the request of the vicar to illustrate his sermon for harvest.

"Jesus" in the languages of the world.   *Biggin Hill Christian Fellowship*

Two appliqué banners made for 'New Wine Bible week.'   *St Andrews, Chorleywood*

Vine. 3-dimensional effect with garden trellis. Leaves in varied greens, veins stitched and stiffened with garden wire. Hand-embroidered lettering.

Many Parts. Paper banner completed in 1 ½ hours at parish weekend workshop. Random shape letters taken from the words 'many parts' used to create background.

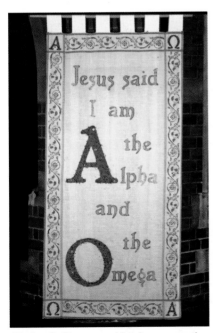

Alpha & Omega. Hand-cut stencil for border, sprayed gold and finished with fabric paints. Illuminated capitals emphasised with mirrorwork.

Harvest. Detailed naive design on green felt. Lettering of machine-knitted cord stiffened with wire.

Banners by St. Gabriel's Cricklewood, London

Bread of Life. 3-dimensional simple design to reflect the subject, with stencilled lettering as used on grain sacks. Fabric paint used for grain.

Light of the World. Inspired by a postcard of fireworks using maribou feathers, fringing, sequin strips and gold spray paint. enhanced with undercoat of orange paint.

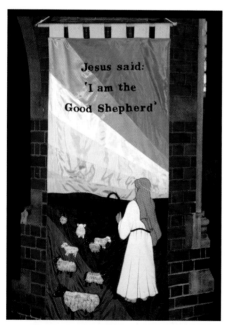

Good Shepherd. Our first banner. Radiating line design intended to increase depth of field. Fine silk background a challenge to work with.

Way, Truth & Life. Simple design in order that the message of the Cross stands out clearly. Shaded ribbons in background. Cross in corduroy.

Banners by St. Gabriel's Cricklewood, London

Banners on the street

Rosas Mitchell, Murray Place Baptist Church, Stirling, Scotland

M arches or processions have become a prominent feature of today's church as the Lord has called us to come and unite with other Christians in our towns and cities to proclaim Jesus.

Our banners are a vital part of this proclamation and will be seen from a distance and possibly on television or in the press.

Banners need to be:

Big, bold and strong

- They must be **simple and clear**. Small decorations will not show up.

- There **must be some large banners** possibly 2-3m wide so that 2 or 3 people can walk between the poles. These very large ones should be interspersed throughout the procession.

- The letters must be very **clear and carefully cut**. Careless letters give a shoddy appearance. Lower case letters are easier to identify at a distance.

- Contrasting colours give boldness and clarity, eg: — white or yellow on black or orange on navy. Primary colours show up well. Good effects can be obtained with fluorescent paper.

March for Jesus, London.

- They must be **prepared to withstand adverse weather conditions**. All types of banners can be sprayed with the appropriate fixer. If there is a strong wind, a few carefully cut holes will allow the air to flow through.

Meaningful

Simple words with a straightforward meaning are best. 'Jesus is Alive', 'Jesus is King', or 'Shine, Jesus, Shine' from the 'Make Way' songs.

Varied

As the procession or march goes by, a variety of banners is effective. They may depict joy, be humorous, or provoke and surprise. Banners can be of all sizes. Hardboard placards can be made by taking a medium size piece of card, using a stencil and spraying through it. Paste the card onto hardboard and nail both to a central stick.

Banners can be mass-produced in different colours in a very short time. Small banners can be made by children. Self-adhesive felt is a useful fabric. An adult can write the letters on the back, backwards, and the child can cut them out and paste them onto card which can then be stapled onto a small garden cane.

Balloons, swivel-sticks, and decorated umbrellas can all add to the fun. Felt doesn't stand up to rain, so if you want your banner to last, use other fabrics such as cotton or crimplene. PVC letters are very bright, waterproof and they do not fray.

Workshops for processions

It is fun to make your banners together in a special workshop session. Prepare your pieces of fabric in advance by machining all the seams. It is a good opportunity to get rid of unwanted gaudy pieces of material. Have a vast selection of fabrics and felts ready and also scissors, glue etc. Workshops can take place about six weeks before the event and then once again nearer the day. Or you may decide to do it all on the morning of the procession!

Provocative banners

Not all banners aim to reassure, encourage or proclaim God's Truth. Some banners can be used to disturb and challenge, to make Christians sit up and think and take action. They can be used powerfully in the right situation and often are needed only once. Sensitivity is required to know that God's message, not merely the views of an individual, is being expressed.

Provocative banners can be used, for example:

- For Good Friday, to bring the message of the Cross.

- For Christian Aid and TEAR Fund days — these might be pictures to make people think about famine, or injustice. A photograph collage of 'Jesus' for TEAR Fund Sunday contained some challenging pictures of Christians in difficult circumstances.

- To remember those persecuted for their faith.

- In 'March for Jesus' marches or processions of witness — perhaps a strong, challenging verse could be used together with proclaiming verses on other banners — such as 'Let justice roll down like water'.

The Spirit of the Lord is on me, because he has anointed me to preach good news to the poor. He has sent me to proclaim freedom for the prisoners and recovery of sight for the blind, to release the oppressed, to proclaim the year of the Lord's favour. Luke 4:18–19

Banners in dance and movement

by Audrey Marriott

I t was about two years ago that I became involved with banners in movement. At that time I heard of Andy Au who had a long experience of dancing with banners and I joined his course. Since then I have felt that the Lord is calling me to use banners in movement to lead his people into freedom and healing of the broken-hearted. Banners can touch dancers deeply as well as lift the worship.

The banners I use are no more than one metre square, or smaller. Polyester lining material or lightweight lurex in plain colours gives the right flare in use. Hardwood

dowel poles are easy to fit into the sleeve and hold one another (see page 13).

Using banners in worship I usually sweep a figure of eight above the head, on each side, at the front or even behind the back. I have also introduced banners alongside scripture, prayer and meditation. For instance, Psalm 23 has very strong verses and the display of two or more colours for each verse as it is read, using different actions brings new depth to the words.

As an alternative to banners, ribbon dancing creates a calming, soothing, light feeling like sparkling water lapping. At times this can be dynamic like rough water cascading over rocks. Large circle movements give a sense of calm and authority and smaller circles a more energetic vibrant one. Even acrobatic moves can be used with ribbons.

A final word — watch out for obstacles such as pew ends, flower stands, candles, pillars and even people!

Where to find materials

Rich coloured and reflective materials can be bought in Asian shops and markets at reasonable prices. Gymnastic ribbons can be bought on a strong wand with a special hook which allows them to rotate easily. I have recently acquired a gymnastic catalogue. (Newton & Co Ltd, Claxton Hall, Malton Road, York YO6 7RE. Tel: 01904 468551.) You can purchase the wands separately and buy your own ribbons. For further information about using banners in dance contact: 'Movement in Worship', City Gate Church, 84-86 London Road, Brighton, West Sussex BN1 4JF.

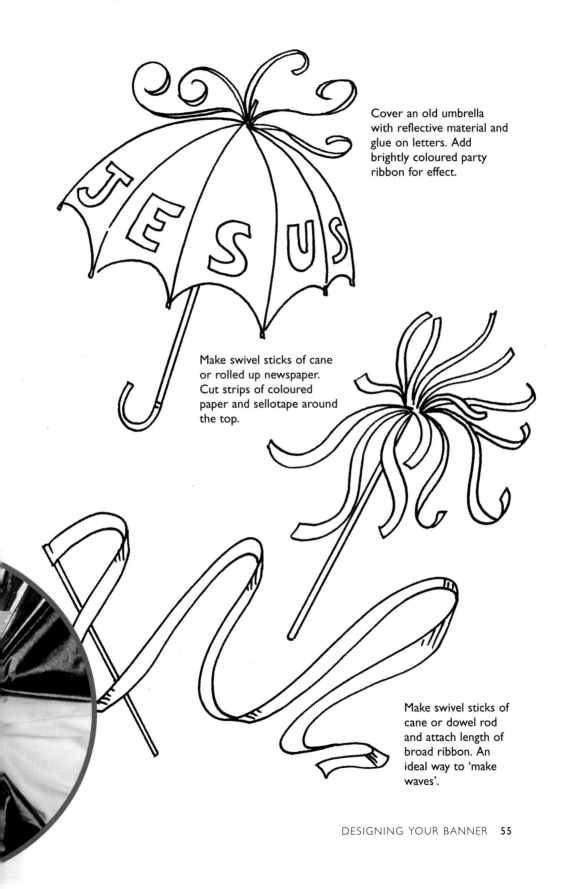

Cover an old umbrella with reflective material and glue on letters. Add brightly coloured party ribbon for effect.

Make swivel sticks of cane or rolled up newspaper. Cut strips of coloured paper and sellotape around the top.

Make swivel sticks of cane or dowel rod and attach length of broad ribbon. An ideal way to 'make waves'.

Making banners with children

We are particularly indebted to Lindy Bairstow of St Paul's, Howell Hill, Cheam, Naomi Lidwell of St Silas Church, Glasgow and Yvonne Davis of Chalfont St Giles, for many of the ideas that follow.

Doing something practical together offers a unique opportunity to foster children's imagination and creativity as well as develop patience and determination, co-operation and respect for the value of each person. It is not only the children who find encouragement in the activity.

> 'It is my opinion that making banners with children is exhausting, exhilarating, challenging and very satisfying, probably in that order! I have often been asked by Sunday Schools, playgroups etc to help make a frieze or similar decoration for an event, and have suggested that we make a banner instead, which is more lasting and which can be re-used.'
>
> **Yvonne Davis,** *Chalfont St Giles Christian Fellowship*

We have heard of banners being made by children ranging from 3 to 13 years of age, sometimes working together in quite large numbers, sometimes in small peer groups. Typically they meet in Play Groups, Sunday Schools, Holiday Clubs and Youth Groups. As well as organised settings, there have been opportunities for individual children to design a banner and then receive help in making it.

There are additional benefits. For instance, children have been thrilled to see their work hanging in the church and to know that their contribution to worship is valued equally with adult banners. In churches where family worship plays a part, displaying children's work emphasises their involvement. Some children's banners have produced more comment than adult ones and in some churches it has been a good way to introduce banners into a church for the first time, as people will readily accept what children have produced. Most importantly, thinking about what to create can be an important milestone in learning to listen to God and ask for the Holy Spirit's help.

The role of the leader and helper

It is essential to have a leader who can plan and prepare; to direct and co-ordinate; assist where necessary; always encourage — and to have plenty of help on hand.

With young children a good number of helpers is vital — one to every two under-fives is recommended. Even with seven to ten-year-olds you need more help than you think!

Planning is important. A collection of junior craft books will give guidelines as to what is appropriate for various age groups and what will spark off new ideas. Often children's designs, though lacking in draughtsmanship, are full of imagination. The role of the group leader is to direct and co-ordinate the proceedings. The leader may feel totally exhausted at the end of a children's banner-making session, but be amazed at what has been achieved!

Materials

- For backgrounds — sheeting, calico, cheap hessian sacking, cotton.
- Coloured materials, lace, felt including self-adhesive felt, fun fabric, ribbon including silver and gold, cord, fringing, wool scraps, sweet papers, milk bottle tops.
- PVA glue.
- Paper or cardboard templates of letters and figures.

Children's pictures drawn with fabric crayons are stuck onto this playgroup banner.

Chalfont St Giles Christian Fellowship, Bucks

Children's drawings enlarged using photocopier and back-stitched using black wool. Felt lettering.

Christchurch, West Croydon

Some basic tips

- Completely finish the 'blank' banner before the session. Children want to see their efforts hung up at once. Plain sheeting and cheap hessian sacking are both effective.
- If there is only one session, the theme, verse and ideas for pictures/design must be thought out beforehand. If more time is available the idea can be just a framework in which the children can do 'their own thing', producing spontaneity and freshness. Ideally the theme should come from the children but this requires more sessions.
- Make sure you have plenty of tasks for all who come.
- Have several complete alphabets of card letters, which can be reversed and drawn round (older children can then cut out and stick on).
- Simplicity is the key to success.

Ideas for projects

It is probably best for the leader to concentrate on a theme — 'Jesus is'…my Saviour, Shepherd, Friend, Light, Healer, Way, Life, Truth, for example. It is also good for the group to spend some time together in worship, if possible led by themselves. The leader's task is to help the children concentrate on one idea and ask the Holy Spirit to give each one a picture. The secret is to be still and listen.

Visual aids are very important in helping children to find imaginative ideas. For example, a picture or an object, photographs of different images. But the ideas for the banner should come from them.

Guidelines

The following points may be of help:

Sizes

If the banner is to be taken home, rather than a joint effort to be hung in church, between one and two feet square is recommended.

Shapes

Visually, rectangles are best, but triangles or circles are possibilities.

Colours

Use a variety of contrasting colours. Experiment with unusual combinations.

Lettering

Keep it bold, simple and free — children learn to read lower case first, not capitals.

> 'Children can create their own designs, given a theme and sometimes pictures or photos to spark them off. I never design banners for adults to make and neither do I for children. Their ideas are often far freer than my own and full of joy and vitality (I also feel that simple ideas work best with good letters cut by an older person using templates.)'
>
> **Yvonne Davis**

The background colour and letters were achieved with coloured paint. The congregation drew round their hands on coloured paper (each hand was signed) and these were cut out and stuck on.
Christchurch, West Croydon

More useful tips

- Use one medium eg paper or fabric.

- Making prints with fabric paints — hands, feet, leaves — is always a success!

- Draw with fabric crayons or fabric painting felt pens on material, and apply the pictures to a background with adhesive. Both these techniques allow for real personal creativity and diversity and are different from the basic collage approach. Felt is easily cut into shapes and crimplene type fabric is also useful because it does not fray.

- A 'quick' banner can be made using spray paint. It is very popular with older boys! Letters for a verse are cut out and stuck on a blank white sheet, sprayed over and then peeled off to reveal the writing in white. We also use self-adhesive felt, expensive but easy to use and gives super results.

Banner-making with young people

by Yvonne Davis

This is the one no one wants to do! Yet, with imagination and buckets full of encouragement, youth have very succinct ways of expressing themselves. I have found myself being intensely moved by the passion of teenagers and have been inspired in my spiritual walk by them. This is not to say that a firm hand is not required, as well as good vocal chords!

The pre-making stage is vital. Some sort of discussion, based on a slide-show, or video, for example is needed to set the scene. Talking the project through and coming up with design sketches can be laborious, but always pays off. The instant answer is rarely the best, and, in this instant age, banner-making can take some putting across — have patience and determination here.

> Teenagers, whether secretly or openly, quite often like the 'subversive feel' of spraying with cans of paint.

A great discovery for me has been spray paint. Teenagers, whether secretly or openly, quite often like the 'subversive feel' of spraying with cans of paint. This realisation has greatly aided me in getting a project going, when I worked with inner-city kids, as well as 'well-churched' young people!

Calico is the best background material. The final design is chalked on and, after plenty of practice, spraying can take place. Needless to say, many plastic groundsheets are required.

The rules are heavily laid down concerning the handling of paint and I have not had an accident yet — even working in Salisbury cathedral. To get a good effect the spray jet has to be close to the fabric as proximity minimises the mess.

We have used car spray paint but other spray paints are available from DIY stores (art shop sprays are ozone friendly). The banners dry in approximately one hour and are then ready to be hung or used in a procession.

I AM: Computer used for lettering — photocopied onto acetate and stencils made and drawn — lettering hand-painted with fabric dye — spray paints used and 'Tulip' paints for outline. This banner took one evening to make.

New Life Church, Woking

Fabric dyes were used to paint this banner and the letters were outlined with 'Tulip' bubble paints. This banner took one evening to make.

New Life Church, Woking

Two 'Free-wheeling' banners. These are spontaneous banners made with speed — usually not symmetrical and done with simplicity and a more casual approach.

Tip
When ironing on letters, cover with greaseproof paper to prevent paint sticking to iron.

Painted background. Fabric letters stuck on with Bondaweb.
New Life Church, Woking

4
Ideas and techniques

In this part we explore different
types of materials and techniques.
Banners featured throughout this book
show how different effects appear

Fabrics and materials

by Yvonne Davis

As a child there was nothing I liked more than to rummage through my mother's scrap bag. I have to admit to the same delight still. Scraps are essential to banner-makers, because you often do not know what you will need until the last moment.

The **background cloth** is very important as it sets the tone of the banner. Cheap stretchy material as a background can ruin the project. I tend to buy firm cloth as the main investment. Fabrics such as corduroy, denim, calico, drill, and so on make excellent backcloths, but lighter fabrics such as polycotton and silk can be used and sometimes interlined. Someone else has commented, 'It is important to have a good weight fabric for the backing! Apart from that ruling, we break all the rules and mix silks, wools, fur fabrics, felts on a banner. A firm backing allows you to do this.'

Squaring up the backing piece of material is important but can be quite difficult. Often the weave isn't straight so one cannot just pull a thread. Although there is a great temptation to rush ahead it is wise to take time to get this first stage right.

Felt is very useful for lettering, is wonderful for cutting intricate shapes and a good range of colours is available. Other fabrics can be obtained by requests in the church bulletin and at jumble sales. **Crimplene** and **PVC** are useful because of their non-fray properties.

Very frayable cloths like lurex and lamé can be stiffened by **ironing on Vilene** to the back. This technique can also work on materials like japsilk and chiffon. Quite a variety of fabrics can be used for largish lettering if it is first backed in this way.

Net can be used to give beautiful effects of water or sky. Several thicknesses create rich colours and ruckled-up white net can create a waterfall. Net needs to be sewn with invisible thread for best effect.

In our banner group we keep colour-coded bags so that all sorts of texture-colour combinations can be easily found. This variety aids design and can add wonderful interest by stimulating new ideas. Another group use storage boxes.

Most of our banners are based on **curtain fabric** and many have felt appliqué so they are not washable. They are for now and we do not feel the need to preserve them for posterity. However, they will probably last a long while. **Scotchguard Spray** can be used to protect the fabric.

A good way to **line a banner** (if it needs it) is to machine the sides like a curtain lining and then turn the top and bottom over and machine or hem in place. A very large banner is best laid face down on the floor with the lining placed on top. Then the edges of the lining should be turned under and stitched in place by hand.

Right: A sample of the huge variety of fabrics and materials available to the banner enthusiast

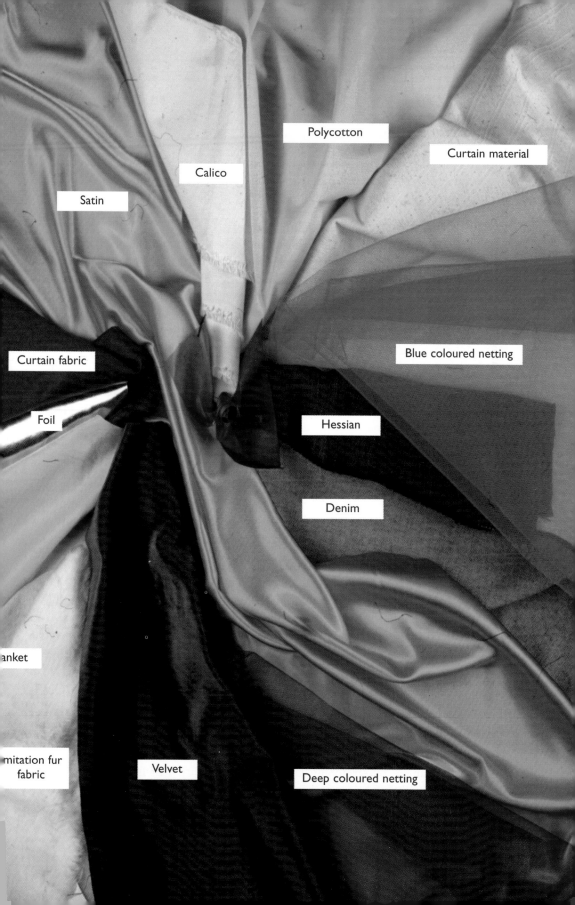

Your questions answered

Should all banners be made to last?

There are no hard and fast rules. Paper and card make attractive banners that will only be used for one or two occasions but in time would become worn. Banners made to last are best made from material to give the design a more enduring quality. These banners will stay in good condition for a number of years.

How do you know what material to use?

For the majority of banners plain materials are best. Velvet and silk are best kept for weddings or for banners of detailed, rich, work. It is hard work stitching felt letters onto velvet. For a quick simple design, cheap fabrics or hessian are appropriate; for a more enduring banner, choose cotton, linen or curtain fabric or other fabrics of a similar quality. Make sure the material is firm enough to hang properly. Both background and figures may be strengthened by iron-on Vilene (see page 69). Thick-weave materials such as tweed are best of all for backgrounds.

Where can you obtain material?

The best source of background fabrics is found at the remnant counter of a curtain fabric shop. There is often a good selection of material at reasonable prices. Friends may be able to supply old curtains and jumble sales may produce some useful finds. (See *Resources* section at end of the book for names and addresses.)

Does it matter which way the material hangs?

Cotton, woven materials and dull and plain fabrics can be hung any way. Some surfaces appear darker or lighter than they really are when placed certain ways. Shot silks especially change depending on the way the fabric is hung. The full beauty and character of any material can be best judged from a distance.

Where do you keep the material?

Odd pieces collected by a group may fill several boxes or bags and it is good if these can be stored in a central place, but if not, in the homes of members. Material can be bought as each banner is planned. It is also advisable to have several pieces of plain fabric in hand that suit your church building. Remember to get the fabric well in advance.

How do you make up the background fabric?

Machine or hem the sides leaving a sleeve (wider space) at the top for the wooden dowel. You can also have a sleeve at the bottom if you think a rod is needed there. This can add weight, and gives your banner a better shape.

How do you make circular banners?

These can be made by stretching fabric over hardboard which has been cut at a hardware shop. Stitch fabric together across the back. Or try a hoop.

Techniques and materials

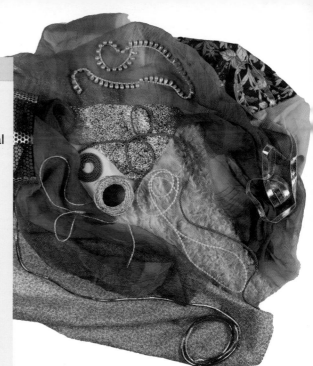

- Appliqué, embroidery and net
- 3-D effects
  - Cord
  - Wool
  - Old jewellery
  - Felt
  - Leather scraps
  - Sequins/buttons
  - Ribbons
- Batik
- Quilting
- Fabric / spray painting on:
  - Foil
  - Lurex
  - Lamé

Vilene
Calico
Cotton
Curtain material
Silk
Satin
PVC
Corduroy
Denim
Drill
Velvet
Scrap materials
Hessian
Blanket
Netting
Organza

How do you make large banners?

- Pin banner under construction to a big block board. Or use an old-fashioned bed as a frame! Use curtain lining, weighted tape or a broom handle as a weight so that the banner hangs well.

How can you make a fringe?

Pull crosswise threads out to form a fringe at the bottom of the background fabric. Alternatively, buy fringe material to suit your banner.

What are the best materials for outdoor banners?

Banners made of cotton and felt can be sprayed with fabric water-proofing (used for tents and raincoats). Remember to make holes somewhere in the centre of the banner to allow air through on a windy day.

How long should banners hang?

This needs to be worked out in each situation — but they should not hang for so long that they lose their impact (except for the very special permanent ones). If you only have a few, have an interval between displaying them.

What about cost?

As banners are part of the life and work of the church, most of us are given the cost of the materials from church funds. The amount is modest compared with many of the other expenses.

How do you store banners?

Rolled up on shelves (possibly slatted), or hung from hooks (possibly extended) in a dry even temperature at the church or at home.

Transferring your design

Y ou're ready to go — you have designed your banner, including the lettering, and chosen the background fabric. You are beginning to have some good ideas of different materials you can use for the banner, and you can't wait to begin.

Gill Douglas suggests the following method: 'Having drawn up your design, trace it onto an overhead projector acetate. Pin a large sheet of paper up on the wall (the reverse of odd pieces of wallpaper will do). Project your image onto the paper and draw round it. You then have a complete paper pattern. Transfer the pattern to the background fabric drawing with tailor's chalk or by using a dressmaker's tracing wheel and carbon paper.' This can be used for larger lettering also.

Priscilla suggests designs can be enlarged on a photocopier. Also designs can be produced on a computer. There is also the more old-fashioned way of 'squaring up'.

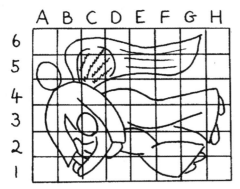

Squaring up a design

Using any ruler, draw squares over your design. Draw the squares again 2 or 3 times the size. Finally, copy your design square by square onto the larger squares (see diagram).

Top: Design drawn on standard sized paper.

Right: Squares drawn so that design is the required size of the banner.

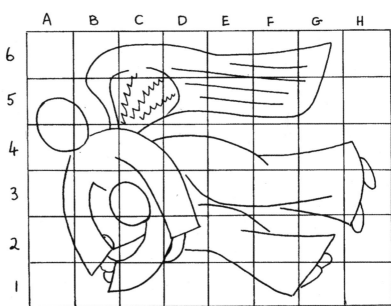

How to create individual letters

1 Draw or trace the letter **2** Scale up to the required size using a photocopier if possible. **3** Cut out the paper letter **4** Draw around it in reverse on the back of the fabric or pin or sellotape the letters to the fabric. **5** Then cut out using sharp scissors. **6** The letters are ready to be pasted or machine-stitched.

Working with words

- **Keep it simple.** It is important that lettering on banners does not get too complicated.

- **Enlarge** lettering on a photocopier to the desired size. A complete alphabet can be enlarged.

- **Typeface.** The Letraset catalogue is full of ideas. There are many books available. It is good to look at several. Use magazine headings as inspiration for lettering style.

- **Scissors as a tool.** When cutting round pen marks on fabric, skill can guide the scissors to more detail and more expressive lettering than the pen could achieve.

- **Delicate lettering.** Make templates for letters and draw round these back to front on self-adhesive labels. Then stick these to the felt and cut both out together. Finally glue or stitch these onto the background.

- **Straight lettering** can be obtained by measuring down the side of the banner, pinning at intervals and running cotton across to act as a guide.

- **Sellotape.** It is better to use sellotape rather than pins in sticking paper letters to felt. They will cut out more accurately.

- **Cord.** Use cord to make flowing lettering. Draw first on the background fabric and oversew the cord onto it.

- **Embroider** round letters or in their centre with chain stitch. Alternatively, attach letters with small buttonhole stitch around the edges and embroider with fly-stitch in the centres. With larger letters use cord around the edge to make them bolder.

- **Iron-on Vilene** is very easy to use:
  1. Use letter templates and trace letters with a fine felt tip pen on to the sticky (shiny) side of the iron-on Vilene — as close together as possible.
  2. Press the material chosen for the letters and then iron on the Vilene in one piece on to the wrong side of the material.
  3. Cut out the letters. The Vilene backing makes the letters easier to handle, helps prevent fraying and if glue is applied thinly and evenly to the bonded material, it doesn't seep through the material so much.

Questions about Lettering

How many words can you have?

This can vary from one word such as 'Rejoice', 'Come', 'Go', and two or three such as 'Fear not', 'Jesus lives' or 'Follow Me' to a much larger number. Up to about seven words can be written in large letters. A longer sentence can be made, but then the letters used should be lower case so that the writing can be read easily. It is very important that the words should be in a colour that shows clearly against the background.

Which glue do I use?

You need to find out which you prefer. Marvin PVA glue is good. UHU and Bostik are very quick to stick. There are more expensive fabric glues available. Glue Gun from America, but available here, has been found useful. Stitchless Glue from George Weil (see *Resources*) enables you to transfer colour pictures from magazines etc to fabric.

Is there any easy way for lettering?

One of the easiest ways is self-adhesive felt. Enlarge letters using overhead projector or photocopier, and stick (sellotape) or pin templates to felt, and cut round (see page 69).

Any ideas for transferring design?

Use embroidery transfer pencils to trace round paper patterns enlarged on overhead projector or photocopy machine. 'Squaring up' works well, but takes time.

Any quick way for detail on plain fabric?

Use fabric marker pen to draw lines instead of stitching.

Using Bondaweb

Bondaweb is excellent for bonding letters and shapes to material. Some banner-makers use it all the time.

It is like double-sided sellotape and is a soft adhesive web attached to a greaseproof paper.

It is very good for bonding thin as well as thicker materials. Lurex, taffeta, silk, silver and gold fabrics can be bonded and the edges are sealed in the process. Full instructions come with the packet.

Using appliqué and embroidery

This is probably the most frequently used method for banners which have a semi-permanent position in a church building or home, and it gives great scope for all sorts of 3D efffects. Appliqué works by sewing shapes of material on to a background. This can be done by hand or by machine. It produces clear and simple decoration and covers large areas quickly. Embroidery using traditional needlework techniques allows the use of different materials, colours, stitches, and so on for different effects.

The pictures and descriptions which follow show some of the lovely effects which can be achieved in these media.

These letters were first drawn on in pencil. Then brown, bobbly, knitting wool was sewn on with an oversewing stitch. The leaves were cut from felt and copied from actual vine leaves in September. The vine leaves were used to make paper patterns.

Coffee-pot banner

Rosemary Woodcock and friends, Downley, High Wycombe

This 'fun' banner was made in the autumn of 1995 for 'Coffee-pot', a new evangelical group for young mums, at The Pastures Church, and designed to hang in their meeting room and convey the ethos in a non-threatening way.

Individual pieces are machine-appliquéd on to an actual tablecloth, and the message is that everyone should feel at home in the group, whoever they are and however they are feeling. The coffee-pot has the word 'JESUS' outlined on it, suggesting that we want to reflect the character of Jesus in everything we do. Around the border are subtly embroidered words:

Jesus said, *'LOVE EACH OTHER AS I HAVE LOVED YOU'*

Sharing: CONCERNS • JOYS • SADNESS • LAUGHTER • TEARS

Offering: FRIENDSHIP • UNDERSTANDING • SUPPORT • ENCOURAGEMENT • COMFORT • HOPE

Avoiding: GOSSIP • CRITICISM • QUARRELS • CLIQUES

Left: Note detail of the name "Jesus" on the coffee pot.

An Easter banner

This was the second in a series of three matching banners (3 ft x 4 ft) made for Good Friday, Easter Day and Pentecost in 1995. The riot of spring flowers is an appliqué of brightly coloured felts glued to a coarse natural hessian background. The crown of glory, made of rich gold vinyl cloth, replaces the crown of thorns on the Good Friday banner. It gives way to a shadowy gold mesh crown which appears faintly in the flames of the Pentecost banner (not illustrated).

Right: detail of the crown and spring flowers clearly showing the three dimensional effect of the petals and the reflective quality of the crown.

The Pastures Church, Downley, High Wycombe

I am the true Vine . . .

These twin banners were designed as one whole. The appliqué on these banners was done entirely by hand. The banner-makers used some interesting fabric for the vine leaves: some of them were made of tie and dye material in shades of green, yellow, white and tan; others were in plain colours in velvet and a silky material. They were backed with iron-on vilene and were attached to the background with gold chain stitch, which runs down the main veins of the leaves so the edges are free and give a 3-D effect. The grapes are circles of taffeta in various colours, gathered round the edge and stuffed. They were sewn individually on to a canvas base and then attached to the banner.

St Mary's, Maidenhead, Berks

'My Beloved Son'

by Mary Davis

The inspiration for this banner came from Matthew 3:16–17 in the Authorized Version, describing the baptism of Jesus. '…and He saw the Spirit of God descending like a dove, and lighting upon Him; And a voice from heaven saying, "This is my beloved Son, in whom I am well pleased." '

I felt a need to depict the power of the Holy Spirit, together with the voice of God. This strong feeling of power coming down is represented by the descending doves coming to rest on the baptismal waters. This power was so strong in my mind that it dominated the whole scene and I felt that to show the figure of Jesus would have weakened the design. Instead, I used the rather strong swirling lettering of the title to give a focus on which to rest one's eyes. I 'felt' the design for this banner. I did not sit down with pencil and ruler and try to work out geometrically how I could illustrate the 'power' or the 'voice'. I could almost physically feel the weight and hear the sound and so the design flowed quite naturally.

The central dove has such strength and movement in its swooping position and yet if you close in on that one dove, it has a real look of delicacy and innocence with its soft blue sequinned eye and pearlised feathers. The silver threads from each wing woven through the net background help to centralise the doves as if they come from one place and this triangular effect is reflected in the water.

The suggestion of the shimmering water needed to be no larger than it is. Its shape not only reciprocates the shape of the descending doves but adds depth to the design and illuminates the place where Jesus stood. From a practical point of view the sequinned material would have been too heavy (and too expensive) to cover the lower half of the banner.

In the initial stages the title lettering was neatened and given a 'style' for me by a professional graphic artist. It is very bold writing and has a real flair about it. Consequently I chose white satin bias to help facilitate this flow and appliquéd it by hand onto the net.

The background is formed by many layers of blue and turquoise net. The layers were individually hand-sewn onto a white cotton backing so that I was able to get this graduation in colour from sea to sky without an obvious horizon. To obtain the effect of distance the doves were appliquéd under different layers of net. The central dove is padded, quilted, embellished with beads and sequins and appliquéd on top of all layers. Tassels hang from the top at either side.

The banner can be mounted on its independent stand and has been used to illustrate other themes such as the Holy Spirit and the life of Christ.

Machine embroidery & appliqué

This method of making banners is very satisfying, but you need to plan carefully before you begin sewing.

Gwenda Young suggests the following stages:
1. Tack all pieces into place, pad if necessary for raised effect.
2. Hang in position to see effect and correct if necessary.
3. Machine with zigzag stitching using different coloured thread.
4. Work upwards always to avoid puckering.
5. Work from first layers and untack when picture is complete.

Achieving pleasing 3-D effects

1. Pad shapes with cotton wool and wadding.
2. Use cord to give outlines.
3. Use one colour on top of another to give shadow or 3-D effect on large letters. Offset letters to give desired effect.
4. Use several layers of net to give depth.
5. Stitch on shapes which stick out from the design.
6. Ruckle up material to create a rough surface.
7. Use sequins and beads. These reflect well in artificial light. Large beads can be held in place by a criss-cross of threads.
8. Use different types of fabric.
9. Use several contrasting layers of material to build up a picture.
10. Use wool. This can be couched on to form the bark on a tree trunk to make the hay in a manger, or to make letters.

Using batik

Batik is not difficult. Just remember to get the wax hot enough so that it permeates the cloth. It is not particularly messy either. You can do it any time of the year if you have somewhere to hang wet dyed cloth.

Jane Coulson of The King's Church, Amersham, tells the story of two banners using batik.

We usually meet in a school hall, and the banners are a focal point, giving direction and encouragement. The essence of our work is to capture what is in the Lord's heart for His people.

The banner 'Behold I make all things new' was our first attempt at batik. I wanted to show a fountain and the only way I could think of to achieve the very light effect of the fountain was batik. We first chose the cloth, a remnant of creamy textured synthetic fabric similar to dupion. We then applied hot wax from a saucepan. (Use a sugar

Batik provides a glowing representation of praising hands, a window and a cross; a focal point in a place of worship. *The King's Church, Amersham*

thermometer if possible. The wax should be 120° — 140° C). You can buy batik wax but it will also work with paraffin wax. The wax could be applied with a special *tjanting* spoon or you may find a paintbrush just as good. Both beeswax and the tjanting spoon can be obtained from a good craft shop.

You will need:
- Light coloured cloth, cotton or synthetic, hot wax and saucepan;
- Sugar thermometer if you have one;
- Paint brush or *tjanting* spoon;
- Cold dyes and large brush.

All these can be obtained from a good craft shop.

When all design was waxed on, the cloth was dipped into a bath of cold blue dye and then hung outside, upside down. More dye was then frequently brushed on the bottom half (top when right way round) with a large decorating brush to give a deepening colour, getting darker towards the top of the banner. This was to create the illusion of light in the centre.

used white kitchen paper because newsprint does run off a little. The lettering, which had been waxed on at the same time as the design, was outlined with blue and green felt pen for emphasis. Finally we applied silver lamé, silver thread, crystal drops from an old necklace and some sequins for the water, navy-blue fabric rocks and embroidered moss.

Quilting

These two traditional needlework methods can be used more effectively for banners, giving a 3-D effect, and providing some interesting contrasts of shapes and textures.

Symbolism and colour on an Easter banner
by Priscilla Nunnerley

'God was in Christ reconciling the world unto Himself.' This banner on the great theme of reconciliation was made for Lent.

A visit to Iona inspired the Celtic cross and much later we discovered that this cross stands for love and eternity. The circular arrangement of the words convey the eternal nature of God. The circle and cross suggest God in Christ breaking in to redeem man into the completeness of His own nature and plan.

We chose grey for the cross, a link with the Celtic stone. Green was chosen as the best background for the cross and red for the letters. Much later I learnt that green symbolises life and growth and red the humanity of Christ.

The cross was quilted in grey machine stitching on a shiny grey lining material over a piece

The King's Church, Amersham

of old blanket. The pattern of the stitching was a simple adaptation of the patterns on the Iona crosses. The quilting was pinned and tacked first with the blanket between two layers of lining.

In the centre of the cross are three circles, representing the Trinity, and made with beads and sequins.

Using paints

by Avril Norton of Biggin Hill Christian Fellowship

Spray paints

Spray paint must be used outside or in a well-ventilated room.

There is a wide range of different sorts of paint, which will achieve different effects, at different costs. This chapter is a guide to them. The projects which follow show how they can be used.

Although car aerosol spray paints have a good effect it is better to use ozone-friendly spray paints or other spirit-based ones (from an art and craft shop). For variations in colour, mix and overlap sprays with or without masking a stencil. Use sprays outside on a still day or in a well-ventilated room. Cut newspaper or card to protect all areas not being painted.

> **You will need:**
> - Pale yellow sheets (or other pastel colours)
> - Spray paint
> - Templates of shapes
> - Iron-on Vilene
> - Glue
>
> All these can be obtained from a good craft shop.

Acrylic paints

These paints are water- or PVA-soluble and are quick drying. Try Rowney's CrylaColor. We have used them in several ways:

- Painting directly onto fabric with a brush (use a good quality one). This method can be used on colour fabric, for shading, and as a base for stitching.

- Printing onto fabric, using pieces of wood, cork, polystyrene, string, corrugated card rolled end on or torn to get rib effects. Experiment! The textured effects can be excellent ie wood grain, stone walls, pebble paths etc.

- Spraying. Make up a thin mixture of the colour required in a small bottle (we use perm lotion bottles). Use a metal mouth diffuser to blow the paint onto the banner. You can buy these at art shops. Practise first onto newspaper. The effects vary depending on how hard you blow and how close to the banner you are, but generally give a more spotty effect than aerosol sprays. Do remember to take it easy, and breathe in a lot of fresh air yourself!

Fabric paints

Most widely available are Dylon, Deka, Pelikan and Seta. They are all slightly different so experiment with what you can buy, being careful about mixing colours from different ranges. Most are used directly onto the fabric and then are fixed on by ironing. You need to consider whether the fabric you use will take a hot iron.

Several fabric marker pens are also available and ordinary felt pens can be used. Check to see whether they run. Fabricrayons are used to draw onto paper which is then ironed onto fabric.

Tri-Chem paints come in a wide range of colours — plain, sparkly and puff-effect. The paint is in a tube with a ball-point end and is used rather like a biro. It is a very long-lasting and washable. The paints can be used to fill in large areas of colour, to add areas of shade, texture and pattern. They are particularly useful for adding fine detail (facial features, parts of flowers etc) and for outlining and sharpening edges.

Painting on silk or cotton

by Tessa Spanton

Beautiful backgrounds for banners can easily be created using fabric paints on silk or cotton. Painting on silk gives lovely translucent colours which can be merged. This is useful for skies, water and landscapes. Alternatively this can be done on cotton which is cheaper and usually stronger, but the colours will not be as glowing. With a little practice, motifs and lettering can be painted too, by outlining them with a waterproof line. This is rather like piping lines of icing onto a cake!

All the basic materials you need and a lot more besides are available by mail order from George Weil (see *Resources* section at end of the book).

> **You will need:**
> - A frame
> - Special silk paints
> - Silk fabric (some silks need washing first to remove any dressing)
> - Brushes, pencil or light fade-away pen, drawing pins, gutta — colourless (gold or silver also available)
> - Salt
> - Sellotape.

Stages in silk painting

1. Stretching the silk onto a frame

Purpose-made adjustable wooden frames are best, but you can experiment by using a picture frame, embroidery frame or even a margarine tub or a jam jar and rubber

Drawing the design.

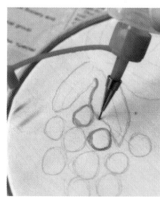

Outlining with gutta.

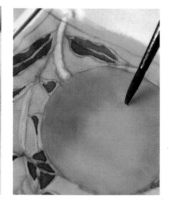

Filling in the colour.

band! It is a good idea to cover a wooden frame with sellotape for easy cleaning afterwards. Now stretch the silk tightly and pin to the frame at two-inch intervals.

2. Transferring the design to the silk

Draw your design on paper with black marker pen then place this under the silk. Trace the design directly using a soft pencil or fade-away marker pen.

3. Outlining the design

As paint spreads rapidly when applied to silk, the design can be outlined with a waterproof line of gutta to keep colours separate. Gutta is applied from a tube with a nozzle or a metal-tipped applicator bottle, then left to dry for about thirty minutes. Instead of gutta you can use a metallic waterproof marker pen.

4. Applying the silk paint

Now you are ready to paint. Fill the areas you have blocked off with paint, letting it spread towards the gutta lines. Watch out for leaks — breaks in the gutta line can be repaired with more gutta. For special effects, see below under 'Water-colour method'.

5. Fixing colours

Water-based colours are fixed by ironing on the back for two to three minutes to make the colours permanent. Finally, rinse in water to remove gutta lines.

Tips for painting on silk or cotton

- For large banners you may need to improvise when it comes to finding a frame. Try stretching your fabric between two tables, fixing with masking or parcel tape. Or attach strong cords to each corner of your fabric, and stretch between garden stakes, trees, furniture etc.

- Lettering can be done by outlining with gutta. Dry the paint immediately using a hair dryer to minimise any problems with leaks.

- For a quick colourful background, cover a large table with polythene, lay your fabric on it, and secure the edges with masking tape. Wet but do not saturate the fabric, then apply colours, letting them merge. You can use salt, but do not use gutta, as it will stick to the polythene, and you will not get a good line. Fabric letters and motifs can be added using *Bondaweb*.

Two examples of painting on silk using gutta.

Water-colour method

Using a large paintbrush or sponge, moisten but do not saturate the silk. Rapidly apply the colours to the wet silk so that they run and blend into each other. Lighter streaks can be achieved by stroking the damp paint with a moist cotton wool bud or shade with a damp brush to get soft edges. If you do not want the colours to blend, let one dry before adding another.

To create a marbled effect, sprinkle the wet paint with fine or coarse salt crystals. Drops of water or alcohol dropped onto wet paint can also make interesting patterns. Lay objects on the wet paint ie, leaves, lace, stencils etc. Remove when the silk is dry. If you do not want the colours to spread, dye thickener can be added to the paint, or the silk can be treated first with an anti-spread product. This is useful for fine details.

A quick banner

Method

- Cover a large table with thick polythene.

- Lay the fabric on the polythene, and secure the edges with masking tape.

- Wet, but do not saturate, the fabric using a household brush or sponge. Blot off any excess water with kitchen paper.

You will need:
- Silk paints; yellow, orange, red
- Polythene sheet
- Masking tape
- Household paint brush or sponge
- Bondaweb
- Background fabric: cotton or silk 70 x 35cm
- Fabric for letters.

- Using the 'landscape' format, rapidly cover the top third of the fabric with yellow paint. Below this, and slightly overlapping with the yellow, apply orange paint to the next third, and in the same way, red to the bottom third. Where the colours meet, you can leave them to mix or blend them with your brush. Make some lighter streaks by stroking across the wet paint with a small sponge, cotton wool ball or screwed up tissue.

- Leave to dry then iron on the reverse to fix. Attach fabric letters to the silk with Bondaweb.

- Finish by hemming the edges or lining. If you used a thin silk, mount it by stretching it over a piece of plywood or chipboard, and stretching on the back with a strong adhesive tape.

Getting prepared for making a quick banner outside.

More banner techniques

Crayons, paint and dye

Exodus — Crossing the Red Sea
The background (thermal curtain lining) was dyed batik-style with wax in between colours, (fabric dyes or paints) to give definition. 'Tulip' paints were used to create the image of the fire going ahead and acrylic car paints for the cloud behind, fabric crayons for the people, background thermal curtain lining (calico could have been used).

New Life Church, Woking

Painted banners

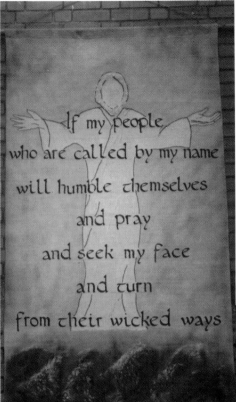

Templates were cut with a craft knife for the figure and text. A paint diffuser was used for the yellow of the aura and the blue of the sky. The text was stencilled in maroon fabric paint and turbulence painted by hand. Folds of fabric and hair were couched with thick wool.

Three templates were cut for cloud formation, the land and the text. A paint diffuser was used for the sky. The text and outline of buildings were stencilled with fabric paint and highlights were applied with couched wool.

These large banners were made by Jennifer Ashdown and friends.
St Andrews, Chorleywood, Herts

Mixed-media banners

The background is blue linen and the centre of the sun dyed silk. The rays are patch dying underneath, then coloured nets, then lines of sequins.

Christchurch, Woking

A wedding banner. The theme of the wedding was sunflowers and the banner was made to match. Top section batik. Bottom section appliqué.

Rosas Mitchell, Anne Dryer

Cotton and net banners

Felt and cord

The daffodils are made by stitching the petals to a central tube — all felt material. A border was added to this banner.

A three dimensional effect is achieved by glueing individual flowers to a fabric background. The outline of the cross is achieved using cord hand-stitched to the background.

GIVE THANKS TO THE RISEN LORD

Dove designs

The dove side on represents peace, the vertical dove the Holy Spirit.

Use cotton or silk fabrics with embroidery or decoration of beads, buttons or jewels.

Wadding can be used to give a 3D effect. See also page 75.

From Scotland

West Wickham Baptist Church

From Scotland

Experimenting with embroidery

Samplers supplied by Margaret Farrell

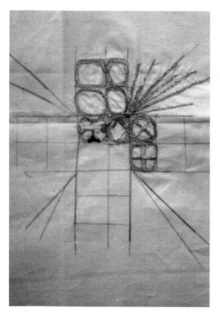

Machine embroidery on calico.

Experimental machine embroidery.

Machine embroidery on silk.

Experimental machine embroidery on insulation foil.

Beads, buttons and jewels

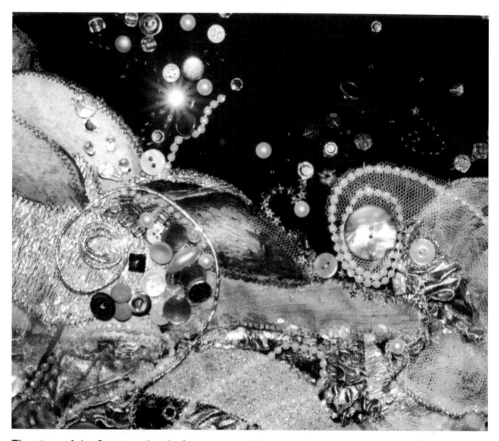

The river of the Spirit — detail of waves on rocks.

St Stephens, East Twickenham

Sponge printing

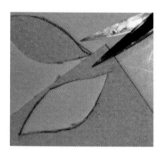 

Specialist compressed sponge for sponge printing on fabric or paper (available from craft shops).

Simply cut out the shape, dip into water and your sponge appears before your eyes.

Banner display ideas

Wall mounted banner. Use a length of dowel rod and carve grooves approx 3cms in from either end for knotting string or wire. Use medium sandpaper to smooth the edges. Use a plumb-line or spirit level to ensure straightness.

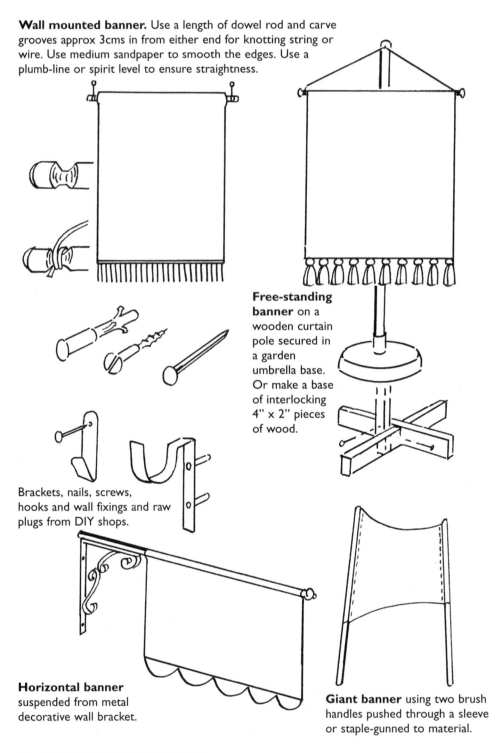

Free-standing banner on a wooden curtain pole secured in a garden umbrella base. Or make a base of interlocking 4" x 2" pieces of wood.

Brackets, nails, screws, hooks and wall fixings and raw plugs from DIY shops.

Horizontal banner suspended from metal decorative wall bracket.

Giant banner using two brush handles pushed through a sleeve or staple-gunned to material.

The future of banners

The use of new technology, lighting and the many fabrics now available vastly increases possibilities for the banner maker. It is a great privilege and also exciting to receive words and pictures from God which can enrich others and bring glory to God at the same time.

Why not consider starting your own banner group? If you already have one and have created some banners why not share a few with people overseas or make one specially for them (see *Banners around the World*).

Gazelle Books intends to publish further Banner books, so please send in banner pictures and stories of your group. Your contribution will be kept and may be considered for entry in future productions. Please send them to:

> The Editor
> Gazelle Books
> Concorde House
> Grenville Place
> Mill Hill
> London NW7 3SA

1996 March for Jesus in Trafalgar Square, London.

Resources

Listed below are some of the tried and tested sources for materials in the UK, as well as some books which you may find helpful.

Sources in the United Kingdom

We suggest you take opportunities to search out some suitable shops when travelling further afield. Look in the yellow pages under Arts and Crafts — visit John Lewis and other big stores — local markets — Asian markets — jumble sales. Ask friends for unwanted silks, materials, necklaces, plain curtains.

Borovick Fabrics is an Aladdin's cave of thousands of fabrics supplied for fashion, stage, screen and TV and church needlework. They only supply fabrics. There is no catalogue but write, with specific details of the type of fabric, colour and use sending a SAE. They will send samples with prices and widths. Then you order sending the payment. S. Borovick, 16 Berwick Street, London W1V 4HP. Tel: 0171 437 2180/0520.

Silk Fabrics – Packs of silk fabric may be obtained from the Silk Route Collection. Write or phone 'The Silk Route', 32 Wolseley Road, Godalming, Surrey, GU7 3EA Tel: 01483 420544

Image House Processing Ltd. Very reasonable sticky prints from your negatives or prints. Ideal for greeting cards. Unit B Astra Business Centre, Roman Way, Ribbleton, Preston, Lancs PR2 5AP. Tel: 01772 652777.

Whaleys (Bradford) Ltd supply silks, cotton, silk and other materials for dyeing and printing, calico, canvas, linen, wadding etc. Send stamp for catalogue to Whaleys (Bradford) Ltd, Harris Court, Great Horton, Bradford, West Yorkshire BD7 4EQ. Tel: 01274 576718. Minimum order £15.00.

Oliver Twists. Hand-dyed threads, fibres and fabrics, experimental collage packs. All sorts of unusual items for traditional and creative embroiderers. Large pieces of material dyed to order. Mail order. Send £1 or four first class stamps with SAE to 34 Holmlands Park, Chester-le-Street, Co. Durham DH3 3PJ.

Colour Prints for Cards (some groups have made cards and bookmarks with photos of their banners). An A4 colour photo copy costs about £1.00. You can copy 4 prints together and cut them up to stick on home-made cards. Most towns have a shop with this service.

George Weil Silk Supplies. Mail order or callers at 18 Hanson Street, London W1P 7DB. Tel: 0171 580 3763. Large suppliers of fabric arts — paints, dyes — screen prints, silk and cotton materials.

Reeves Dryad — for sticky-backed felt. 178 Kensington High Street, London. Tel: 0171 937 5370.